THE GOSPEL FOR LIFE

SERIES

THE GOSPEL &

Marriage

Also in the *Gospel for Life* series

THE GOSPEL FOR LIFE

SERIES

THE GOSPEL &

Marriage

SERIES EDITORS

RUSSELL MOORE *and*
ANDREW T. WALKER

PUBLISHING GROUP

NASHVILLE, TENNESSEE

978-1-4336-9043-3

Published by B&H Publishing Group
Nashville, Tennessee

Dewey Decimal Classification: 306.81
Subject Heading: BIBLE. N.T. GOSPELS \ MARRIAGE \
DOMESTIC RELATIONS

1 2 3 4 5 6 7 8 • 21 20 19 18 17

CONTENTS

- *Focus on Pleasing Your Spouse (Not Yourself)*
- *Be Lavish in Your Forgiveness*
- *Living according to the 100/100 Plan*
- *Pray Together Every Day as a Couple*
- *Build a Relationship That Will Outlast Your Parenting Years*
- *Fulfill Your Unique Roles and Responsibilities*
- *Rely on God during Times of Hardship and Suffering*
- *Develop a Common Mission*

Series Preface

Russell Moore

Why Should the *Gospel for Life* Series Matter to Churches?

IN ACTS CHAPTER 2, WE READ ABOUT THE DAY OF PENTECOST, the day when the resurrected Lord Jesus Christ sent the Holy Spirit from heaven onto His church. The Day of Pentecost was a spectacular day—there were manifestations of fire, languages being spoken by people who didn't know them, and thousands of unbelievers coming to faith in this recently resurrected Messiah. Reading this passage, we go from account to account of heavenly shock and awe, and yet the passage ends in an unexpectedly simple way: "And they devoted themselves to the apostles' teaching, to the fellowship, to the breaking of bread, and to the prayers" (Acts 2:42 ESV).

I believe one thing the Holy Spirit wants us to understand from this is that these "ordinary" things are not less spectacular than what preceded them—in fact, they may be more so. The disciplines of discipleship, fellowship, community, and prayer are the signs that tell us the kingdom of Christ is here. That means that for Christians, the most crucial moments in our walk with Jesus Christ don't happen in the thrill of "spiritual highs." They happen in the common hum of everyday life in quiet, faithful obedience to Christ.

That's what the *Gospel for Life* series is about: taking the truths of Scripture, the story of our redemption and adoption by a risen Lord Jesus, and applying them to the questions and situations that we all face in the ordinary course of life.

Our hope is that churches will not merely find these books interesting, but also helpful. The *Gospel for Life* series is meant to assist pastors and church leaders to answer urgent questions that people are asking, questions that the church isn't always immediately ready to answer. Whether in a counseling session or alongside a sermon series, these books are intended to come alongside church leaders in discipling members to see their lives with a Kingdom mentality.

Believers don't live the Christian life in isolation but rather as part of a gospel community, the church. That's why we have structured the *Gospel for Life* series to be easily utilized in anything from a small group study context to a new member or new believer class. None of us can live worthy of the gospel by ourselves and, thankfully, none have to.

Why are we so preoccupied with the idea of living life by and through the gospel? The answer is actually quite simple: because the gospel changes everything. The gospel isn't a mere theological inquiry or a political idea, though it shapes both our theology and our politics. The gospel is the Good News that there is a Kingdom far above and beyond the borders of this world, where death is dead and sin and sorrow cease. The gospel is about how God brings this Kingdom to us by reconciling us to Himself through Christ.

That means two things. First, it means the gospel fulfills the hopes that our idols have promised and betrayed. The Scripture says that all God's promises are yes in Jesus (2 Cor. 1:20). As sinful human beings, we all tend to think what we really want is freedom from authority, inheritance without obedience like the prodigal son. But what Jesus offers is the authority we were designed to live under, an inheritance we by no means deserve to share, and the freedom that truly satisfies our souls.

Second, this means that the gospel isn't just the start of the Christian life but rather the vehicle that carries it along. The gospel is about the daily reality of living as an adopted child of a resurrected Father-King, whose Kingdom is here and is still coming. By looking at our jobs, our marriages, our families, our government, and the entire universe through a gospel lens, we live differently. We will work and marry and vote with a Kingdom mind-set, one that prioritizes the permanent things of

Christ above the fleeting pleasures of sin and the vaporous things of this world.

The *Gospel for Life* series is about helping Christians and churches navigate life in the Kingdom while we wait for the return of its King and its ultimate consummation. The stakes are high. To get the gospel wrong when it comes to marriage can lead to a generation's worth of confusion about what marriage even is. To get the gospel wrong on adoption can leave millions of "unwanted" children at the mercy of ruthless sex traffickers and callous abusers. There's no safe space in the universe where getting the gospel wrong will be merely an academic blunder. That's why these books exist—to help you and your church understand what the gospel is and what it means for life.

Theology doesn't just think; it walks, weeps, and bleeds. The *Gospel for Life* series is a resource intended to help Christians see their theology do just that. When you see all of life from the perspective of the Kingdom, everything changes. It's not just about miraculous moments or intense religious experiences. Our gospel is indeed miraculous, but as the disciples in Acts learned, it's also a gospel of the ordinary.

Introduction

Andrew T. Walker

I LIKE TO CALL MARRIAGE THE GREAT "UNEXAMINED ASSUMPTION" of our time. Nearly everyone around us aspires to marriage and will in fact get married. Marriage it seems is a simple fact of our existence. It's the one institution that brings together men and women to be husbands and wives and turns them into fathers and mothers. Marriage and family life are the very axis upon which the fortunes of society turn. But does that mean that we as Christians, and American culture, have gotten marriage right? Sadly, no.

Statistics paint a pretty bleak picture about the reality of marriage. People are marrying later in life. Fewer marriages are taking place. Cohabitation has assumed the role that marriage once provided. Divorce is still commonplace in America. And now, the very notion of marriage—the idea that marriage is a gendered institution between men and women—has been turned on its head by a wrongly decided Supreme Court case. Marriage is in disarray, and in a state of free fall.

Yet, the idea of marriage is still an enchanted institution in America. Little girls dream of their wedding day adorned in flowing white gowns. Teenage boys visualize what they imagine it will be like when their bride comes gracefully down the aisle to exchange vows. No young married couple hopes or foresees divorce. They envision wrinkled hands, interlocked until one spouse passes away.

There's a gap from how we talk about marriage and what we experience in marriage. Our expectations fall short of the ideal, based on the evidence of how marriage is fairing across the American landscape.

Marriage in America needs help. It needs re-examination. Since marriage has always been with us, many of us have never had to ask tough questions like: What is it for? Why did God give us marriage? What's the recipe for a successful marriage?

It also needs re-enchantment as an institution that unites men and women, pictures what God is doing in Christ, and helps serve as a foundation for society. In this short book on marriage, we've assembled a team of writers, practitioners, pastors, and scholars to help reframe the subject of marriage along those very lines.

Each book in the *Gospel for Life* series is structured the same: What are we for? What does the gospel say? How should the

Christian live? How should the church engage? What does the culture say?

The Gospel for Life: Marriage is intended to be an introductory look at how Christians should engage marriage from every angle of the Christian's life—their place in culture, their engagement as everyday Christians, and their role in the body of Christ—the church. We want no stone unturned when talking about how the gospel of Jesus Christ shapes us as a people on mission for God in every sphere of our life—not least of which is marriage, the one institution where most people will find themselves for forty to even sixty years.

We hope that you'll pick this book up and that its contents will question your assumptions, and perhaps reveal to you incorrect thinking about how Christians have too passively consumed the culture's vision of marriage to the exclusion of the biblical vision of marriage. Most importantly, we hope to show you how marriage reflects the greatest truth of the world—the gospel of Jesus Christ, and how the centrality of the gospel transforms marriage.

What Are We For?

Mary Kassian

FIFTY YEARS OF MARRIAGE IS TRADITIONALLY CALLED ONE'S Golden Anniversary. You probably knew that. Sixty years is one's Diamond Anniversary. Maybe you knew that too. But did you know that a man and woman who have been married for sixty-five years get to celebrate their Blue Sapphire Anniversary? I'm privy to that tidbit of information because I recently hosted a massive celebration for my parents' sixty-fifth.

Wow! Sixty-five years of marriage (and counting) is a significant accomplishment. My husband and I have barely been married half that long. And with a scant thirty-three years' experience under my belt, my eighty-seven-year-old mother is quick to remind me that when it comes to marriage, I still have a lot to learn.

Scripture contains numerous truths about marriage. One has only to scan its opening pages to discover that marriage is, first and foremost, utterly and undeniably God's idea.

Marriage Is God's Notion

"He who created them in the beginning made them
male and female . . . [husband and wife]." (Matt. 19:4)

Genesis 1 gives us a broad overview of humanity's creation. It informs us that God created man in His own image; male and female He created them. He blessed the newlyweds and gave them the mandate to be fruitful and multiply (Gen. 1:27–28). Genesis 2 rewinds the tape, zooms in, and provides some additional details in slow-motion, as it were. It shows that the Lord God created the male first, from the dust of the ground. He created the female second, from a rib He extracted from the male. It also lets us in on the fact that the Lord created woman as man's perfect counterpart. The wedding was immediate. The man was still standing there gawk-eyed and spouting poetry when God pronounced them husband and wife (Gen. 2:15–23).

No doubt you're familiar with the narrative. But at the risk of stating the obvious, let me make a few observations.

It was *God* who created mankind.

It was *God* who created male and female. He is the one behind the man-woman binary.

It was *God* who created marriage and sex. He was the first Father, metaphorically speaking, to walk a bride down the aisle. He was the first officiant. Marriage followed His creation of man and woman like a clap of thunder after a flash of lightning. It was all part of His plan.

Marriage is not a human construct. God created marriage. And it existed from the get-go. Right from the beginning, it was God's divine purpose that human couples unite in exclusive, indivisible, one-flesh, lifelong covenant relationships. Jesus reiterated this basic fact,

> "Haven't you read," He replied, "that He who created them in the beginning made them male and female," and He also said, "For this reason a man will leave his father and mother, and be joined to his wife, and the two will become one flesh? So they are no longer two, but one flesh. Therefore, what God has joined together, man must not separate." (Matt. 19:4–6)

Christ's words indicate that God is ultimately the one who joins husband and wife together and makes the two one. Think for a moment about the staggering implications. Not only was God the officiant at the first wedding, but marriage is so utterly and completely God's doing, that He stands *de facto* behind each and every covenant. Marriage is sacred, holy, and divine in origin. God not only seals the deal, Malachi indicates that He also breathes "a portion of the Spirit" into each marital union.

> The LORD was witness between you and the wife of your youth . . . she is your companion and your wife by covenant. Did he not make them one, with a portion of the Spirit in their union? (Mal. 2:14–15 ESV)

Marriage is set in motion and defined by God. Its essence is such that it cannot and does not exist outside of God. The institution is so God-created, God-ordained, God-sanctioned, and God-breathed that He stands as the judicial contract-maker and witness at every wedding. That doesn't mean that He condones each person's choice of a marriage partner. But it does mean that whenever a man and a woman marries, God is the end-cause of the joining that takes place. Highly invested in the institution He created, the Lord testifies to each vow. And in His common grace, His breath enlivens every covenant.

Marriage Is Defined by God

Dictionaries used to define *marriage* as "a legally accepted relationship between a man and a woman in which they live as husband and wife." But no longer. The popularization of common-law marriage, the advent of same-sex marriage, and the acceptance of transgender ideology has forced culture to purge sex-specific references such as man and woman, and husband and wife, out of its explanations.

Most dictionaries now define *marriage* as something like this: "a state in which two individuals are wholly committed to live with each other in sexual relationship, under conditions normally approved and witnessed to by their social group or society." According to this rather awkward definition, two people—opposite sex, same sex, transgender, or whatever gender they consider themselves to be—are married if: a) they are sexually involved and committed to maintaining a common residence, b) society as a whole doesn't object to their relationship (as it currently would in cases of incest, for example), and c) someone can attest to the validity of their living arrangement.

I don't know about you, but I grieve at such a shallow view. The Bible presents a vision infinitely more noble, beautiful, and heart-stirring. God's Word flies in the face of the idea that marriage is merely a social custom or an evolving human institution that we can define and redefine at will. Marriage is God's notion, not ours. He purposed it since the beginning. Before the ages even.

In order to rightly understand marriage, we dare not leave God out of it. He must be our starting point. If marriage is God's idea and doing, and if indeed He creates and ratifies the marriage union, then it stands to reason that He's the one who gets to dictate the terms. God—not man—gets to define what marriage is all about.

One of the main aims of this chapter is to summarize how God defines marriage. This is what we are *for*. These are the positive assertions of what marriage, at its essence, is.

There are several good Bible-based definitions out there. *The Baptist Faith and Message 2000* defines *marriage* as "the uniting of one man and one woman in covenant commitment for a lifetime." The definition is short, succinct, and sound. But I'd like to propose a slightly expanded version,

> Marriage is a spiritual and legal covenant between
> two complementary counterparts (one biological
> male and one biological female), through which they
> are joined by God in a one-flesh union, and commit
> to pursue and enjoy a conjugal, exclusive, indivisible,
> lifelong love relationship.

Let's unpack it phrase by phrase. I think each part of the definition accurately reflects what the Bible teaches about the institution. To begin, marriage is *"a spiritual and legal covenant."*

A Spiritual and Legal Covenant . . .

Malachi 2:14 makes it clear that marriage is a covenant relationship. She is "your wife *by covenant*." Proverbs 2:17 maintains that the adulteress "forgets the covenant of her God." Marriage isn't the only type of covenant we see in Scripture, but it's a highly significant one.

What exactly is a covenant? A covenant is a legal, binding interpersonal agreement or commitment that outlines the obligations of each party in a relationship. Often, it outlines the blessings that accompany fulfillment of one's covenant obligations, and warns of the negative consequences (curses) for those who fail to meet them. *A covenant differs from a contract in that it formalizes the terms of a relationship rather than quantifying an interchange of goods or services.* People who enter into a covenant form an unbreakable alliance, association, or bond. Furthermore, unlike a contract, which only requires human witnesses and can be broken, a covenant is a permanent oath that is witnessed and guaranteed by God. It is both legal and spiritual.

According to the Bible, living together in a committed sexual relationship does not alone constitute a marriage. A marriage requires a formal covenant, ratified in the presence of God and other witnesses. It involves public vows, a pledge to fulfill one's marital obligations, and legal registration with the governing authorities.

Between Two . . .

The next phrase specifies that marriage is between *two* individuals. But if God's plan is monogamy, why did several men in the Old Testament have more than one wife? And why on earth did God tolerate it?

Hebrew marriage was essentially monogamous.[1] Polygamy (polygyny) was largely confined to the ruling and upper classes. A ruler would marry multiple wives to secure heirs and/or make political alliances (1 Kings 3:1). Polygamy was practiced by Lamech (Gen. 4:19), Abraham (Gen. 16), Jacob (Gen. 30:1–8), Gideon (Judg. 8:30), King David (1 Sam. 25:39; 2 Sam. 3:2; 5:13), Solomon (1 Kings 9:16; 11:3), and Rehoboam (2 Chron. 11:21). It's important to note that although the Bible reports that certain men had multiple wives, it does not condone the practice. The passages are *descriptive* rather than *prescriptive*. That's an important distinction. Nowhere in the Bible is polygamy ever sanctioned.

Jesus clarified for us that God's design for marriage is one man and one woman, as it was in the beginning. When the Pharisees pressed him about the practice of divorce, Jesus essentially said, "Moses gave you some guidelines because of your sinful hearts, but I'm overruling that concession and calling you to a higher standard, because divorce is not God's plan" (Matt. 19:3–12; Mark 10:2–12, author paraphrase). Had He been asked about polygamy, He would have undoubtedly answered in the same manner.

For Jesus and Paul, and for the church, marriage and sexual ethics are not based on the cultural practices or sins that are reported in the Old Testament, but from the pre-fall monogamous union of man and woman that God instituted at creation.

Complementary Counterparts (one biological male and one biological female) . . .

God's pattern for marriage involves one biological male and one biological female. Genesis is clear that God created two sexes—male and female, and joined these two binary beings in marriage. He did not create any other gender or any other type of marital union. In God's plan, male-female marriage is the only kind of marriage there is.

The phrase "complementary counterparts" is also important. When God created woman, His stated intent was to make "a helper as his complement" (Gen 2:18). In other words, a counterpart to man—matching, but not the same. Literally "like-opposite." In Genesis 2:23 the Hebrew word for man is *ish*, derived from a root meaning "strength" and the word for woman is *ishsha* derived from the root "soft." God's creation of man differed from His creation of woman, as did the final creatures He made.

The New Testament is clear that your biological gender—the sex God gave you before birth—is accompanied with the expectation that you will embrace and not reject His sex-specific design. Your biology equals God's destiny for you. If you are male, your role-responsibility is different from that of a woman. If you are female, your role-responsibility is different from that of a man. Mature manhood requires that a man "step up" to accept responsibility to offer his masculine strength through appropriate and charitable guidance, provision, and protection. Mature womanhood requires that a woman embrace her responsibility to cultivate a nurturing, life-giving, amenable spirit, and to appropriately respond.[2]

These sex-specific responsibilities are particularly important in marriage (see Eph. 5). Male and female are not clones who just happen to have a few different body parts. Although the similarities are vast, God created male and female to be different to the core of our beings. We complement one another (not compliment, although that doesn't hurt either). A complement is "either of two corresponding parts that completes the whole." Like two puzzle pieces, it's a part that has a corresponding part that perfectly matches and fits. When male and female are united in marriage, it's not just the physical parts that correspond and fit together in a complementary way—it's also their roles and responsibilities.

Through Which They Are Joined by God in a One-flesh Union . . .

The complementary differences between man and woman facilitate their union. In marriage, God joins two individuals in a symbiotic way: "And the two will become one flesh. So they are no longer two but one flesh. Therefore, what God has joined together, man must not separate" (Mark 10:8–9).

Note again that it is ultimately God, in a divine act, who effectually does the joining. And in His eyes the net result is a whole new entity—one being, one body, one flesh.

One flesh isn't just a coming together sexually, although it does involve that. The Bible indicates that marriage is an intimate union that involves every aspect of a person's being—spiritual, emotional, physical, financial—thoughts, hopes, dreams, heart, everything. It's a jaw-dropping, mind-blowing concept that God creates a union so deep and complete, that the individual parts are supernaturally eclipsed by the greater whole. In the spiritual realm, two actually become one. This is a great mystery, whose meaning was hinted at, but did not become fully apparent until the coming of Christ. More about that later.

And Commit to Pursue and Enjoy a Conjugal, Exclusive . . .

The sexual act ratifies the deal. Conjugal sex is a beautiful and holy gift. It consummates (completes) the marriage covenant. It illustrates, in the physical realm, that an emotional, spiritual, legal one-flesh union has, in fact, taken place. In the sexual act, a husband and wife affirm in the private realm what has taken place in the public and heavenly realm. They tell and retell the story. Sex is the testimony. Sex bears witness that God has made two one. That's why God restricts sex to marriage and why sex outside of marriage is so offensive to Him. If unmarried individuals are physically intimate, they tell a lie with their bodies. They testify that a divine joining has taken place, when in fact it has not. And since the covenant of marriage was created to bear witness to God's covenant through Jesus, their behavior also tells a lie about God.

Marriage is an exclusive romantic and sexual relationship. Spouses forsake all other alliances and remain faithful to each other. Their relationship and their newly established family unit take highest priority in their lives. Their ties with one another supersede all other family ties. Genesis 2:24 (KJV) says a man "leaves" his father and mother and "cleaves" to his wife. Certainly the woman leaves and cleaves as well, but the emphasis indicates that the man is the one who becomes head of the new family unit, and that he bears a unique responsibility for its success.

The word *cleaves* reflects the central concept of covenant-faithfulness. The Hebrew word *dabaq* suggests the idea of being permanently glued together. It's sometimes translated as "cling" or "hold fast." *Dabaq* is one of the words frequently used to express the covenant commitment of God's people: "Take diligent heed to . . . love the LORD your God, and to walk in all his ways, and to keep his commandments, and to cleave unto him, and to serve him with all your heart and with all your soul" (Josh. 22:5 KJV; see also Deut. 10:20; 11:22; 13:4; 30:20).

Indivisible, Lifelong . . .

It is not in man's power to destroy the uniting that God performs in marriage. "What therefore God hath joined together, let not man put asunder" (Matt. 19:6 KJV). Jesus taught that the marriage bond is so permanent that even a legal divorce cannot break it: "Everyone who divorces his wife and marries another woman commits adultery, and everyone who marries a woman divorced from her husband commits adultery" (Luke 16:18; see also Matt. 5:32; 19:9; Mark 10:11–12).

Christ's view on the permanence of marriage was so stringent that His disciples balked, claiming it was better to forego marriage than to try to live up to such a high standard. But Jesus held firm. He responded, "Let everyone accept this who can" (Matt. 19:12).

Marriage forms an indivisible bond that lasts until the death of one's spouse (Rom. 7:2). When a spouse dies, the marriage is over and the surviving spouse is free to remarry. Some Sadducees (liberal religious academics) thought Christ's views on marriage and the resurrection presented an ideal opportunity to trip Him up. They asked Him about a theoretical situation: "What if a woman gets married and is widowed seven times? In heaven, whose wife will she be?" (Luke 20:27–35, author paraphrase).

Jesus answered that in heaven people "neither marry nor are given in marriage." Marriage was the opening act of human history, but when the curtain falls and time ends, it will be no more

(Luke 20:34–35). It will give way to the eternal reality to which it has pointed all along. (Again, more about that in a moment.)

Love Relationship

Finally, although it may be stating the obvious, I believe it's important to emphasize that marriage is primarily a covenant of love. Marital vows are a commitment by the couple to love, faithfully nurture, invest in, work at, and enjoy their exclusive love relationship until parted by death.

> To have and to hold from this day forward, for better, for worse, for richer, for poorer, in sickness and in health, to love and to cherish, till death us do part, according to God's holy ordinance, in the presence of God I make this vow.

As the pastor normally reminds the couple before they take this oath, "no other human ties are more tender, no other vows are more sacred . . . You are entering into that holy estate which is the deepest mystery of experience, and which is the very sacrament of divine love."

Marriage Is God's Object Lesson

Many weddings in North America are still based on the standard traditional wedding ceremony, whose words I quoted above, and which were originally outlined in the Book of Common

Prayer, published in the mid-1500s by the Church of England. After centuries, the script is still in use. I think it's lasted so long because the words are theologically sound, and thus incredibly powerful. Consider the opening statement,

> Dearly beloved, we are gathered together here in the sight of God, and in the face of this company of witnesses to join together this man and this woman in Holy Matrimony; which is an honorable estate, instituted of God, signifying unto us the mystical union that is between Christ and His Church . . . And therefore, not entered into unadvisedly or lightly, but reverently, discreetly, soberly and in the fear of God, duly considering the causes for which Matrimony was ordained.

We've spent the bulk of this chapter defining what marriage is but have not directly talked about why, or to what end, or for what cause, it exists. I think the classic ceremony hits the nail on the head. Marriage "signifies to us the mystical union that is between Christ and His Church."

The apostle Paul makes the point most clearly in Ephesians 5:31–32, where he quotes the Genesis account about the creation of marriage, and then explains the "mystery" that it has always contained: "'For this reason a man will leave his father and mother and be joined to his wife, and the two will become one flesh.' This mystery is profound, and I am talking about Christ and the church." Ephesians 5 indicates that husbands play a unique role in telling the bridegroom part of the story, and that wives play a unique role in telling that of the bride. God created the temporary, earthly, mortal, love-based covenant of marriage to throw a spotlight on the indescribably magnificent eternal, heavenly, immortal one. Earthly marriage is a foretaste of the coming marriage of the Lamb and was created to illustrate and draw people into that cosmic love-relationship (Rev. 19:7).

Marriage is a covenant, because God's relationship with us is covenant-based. It is between two counterparts, because Jesus and the church are counterparts. Two become one, because God is one, and because we become one with Christ, a part of His body. The covenant precedes the union, because we cannot unite with Christ outside of a covenant relationship. The relationship is indivisible, because God will never leave us or forsake us. It's a relationship that embodies faithfulness, because God is faithful. It is a love relationship because of God's love for us. Every part of marriage was created to point to the spectacular relationship between God and His people.

From the beginning, marriage was a visible object lesson given by God to teach humans about invisible spiritual realities. God created manhood, womanhood, marriage, and sex because He wanted us to have symbols, images, and language powerful enough to convey the idea of who He is and what a relationship with Him is all about. Without them, we'd have a tough time understanding concepts such as desire, love, commitment, fidelity, loyalty, unity, intimacy, oneness, covenant, fatherhood, and family. We'd have a hard time understanding God and the gospel. God gave us these images so that we'd have human thoughts, feelings, experiences, and language adequate and powerful enough to understand and express deep spiritual truths. The visible symbols display and testify about what is unseen. That's why the symbols are so very important.

Marriage was created to display the magnificence of God, and to expand His Kingdom. It exists to exalt Jesus and make a relationship with Him irresistible. That's why it's so important that we think about marriage the way God wants us to think about it, and that we do marriage the way God wants us to do it. And that's also why the enemy of God, Satan, works so hard to corrupt and destroy the true meaning of manhood, womanhood, marriage, and sex.

Scripture is emphatic that who we are as male and female has very little to do with us and very much to do with God. What is manhood about? Displaying the glory of Jesus Christ. What is womanhood about? Displaying the glory of Jesus Christ. What is marriage about? Displaying the glory of Jesus Christ. What is sex about? Displaying the glory of Jesus Christ. What is singleness about? Displaying the glory of Jesus Christ. Married couples shine a light on the cosmic romance by faithfully loving their spouses and remaining true to their covenant vows. Singles shine a light on the cosmic romance by remaining sexually pure and enraptured with Christ. They remind us that earthly marriage is temporary and of secondary importance—like the picture that will be forgotten and shoved into the drawer when the lovers meet face-to-face.

I am so grateful for my parents, who have demonstrated what a marriage covenant is all about—both in their romance with each other, and in their faithful commitment to the greater cosmic romance. They've given me a glimpse at the wonder and beauty of it all.

Mom and Dad have been faithful to their vows and loved each other from their paper (1st), to their tin (10th), to their crystal (15th), to their silver (25th) and pearl (30th), to their gold (50th), and all the way to their blue sapphire (65th) anniversary! Maybe they'll make it to their platinum (70th) or even their jade (75th). I don't know. But whenever the Lord takes them home, I'm confident that they'll arrive at heaven's door with big smiles on their faces. They'll dance a jig, throw their hands up in the air, and shout, "We made it! It wasn't always easy, but with God's help we made it! Through better, through worse, through richer, through poorer, in sickness and in health, we loved and we cherished all the way to the end."

I expect the Lord will smile as He places gleaming crowns on their heads, bedazzled with all kinds of stones and precious metals—crystals, pearls, white silver, gleaming gold, and deep blue sapphires—and best of all, a photo of all the kids, grandkids, and great-grandkids set in a tiny tin locket. And He'll chuckle as my mom blushes and insists that it really is too much—she'd be happy with a crown of daisies. He'll clap my dad on the back and embrace him with the same big-old carpenter hug that Dad passed out at every family gathering. And He'll exclaim, "Well done! Great job, good and faithful ones! Come, enter into My joy!"

And then He'll take them by the hand and lead them into the ballroom prepared for the wedding supper of the Lamb. And Mom and Dad, along with the rest of the gathered throng, will finally experience what marriage is all about.

Discussion Questions

1. Why did God create marriage?
2. Consider the following statement: *"Marriage is set in motion and defined by God. Its essence is such that it cannot and does not exist outside of God."* Do you agree? Why or why not?
3. Which part of the biblical definition of marriage is most abrasive to culture? Why?
4. Why do you think culture wants to change the meaning of marriage?
5. What implications does the meaning of marriage hold for those who are married? What are the implications for those who are unmarried?

CHAPTER

2

What Does the Gospel Say?

Denny Burk

OUR CULTURE HAS EXPERIENCED A MASSIVE MORAL REVOLUTION concerning the nature and meaning of marriage. Ten years ago, same-sex marriage was illegal in every state of the union. Ten years later in 2015, same-sex marriage is a constitutional right in all fifty states. That is a massive amount of change in just ten years. But it would be a mistake to think that our culture's devolution on marriage began in 2015 with a decision from the Supreme Court. Same-sex marriage is not the cause of our times but a sign of our times.

Our culture long ago embraced the sexual revolution of the 1960s and 1970s. Our culture long ago succumbed to the idolatry of sex and the diminishing of marriage. We long ago acquiesced to the ubiquity of the birth control pill and the severing of human sexuality from its connection to children and family. Our culture long ago accepted no-fault divorce and the idea that we can change spouses like we change socks. Our culture long ago consented to the idea that there's no difference between men and women and that gender is a social construct that we learn from culture and not something given to us by God at creation. Our culture has long embraced the idea that gender shouldn't matter when it comes to human sexuality. And so we have a whole generation of young people who see homosexuality as an expression of human diversity and not an expression of human fallenness. No, our culture's devolution didn't begin with a Supreme Court decision affirming gay marriage. This slide has been a long time coming.

And yet the Bible's testimony about the meaning and nature of marriage stands in stark contrast to that of our culture. The apostle Paul says that the "mystery" of marriage is profound, "but I am talking about Christ and the church" (Eph. 5:32). By "mystery," Paul says that the meaning of marriage is something that was once hidden in the Old Testament but that now has been revealed in the gospel. The deepest meaning of marriage is that it is an enacted parable of another marriage—the marriage of Christ to His bride. The story of Christ's marriage to His bride is the gospel story itself. Thus the connection between marriage and the gospel is not accidental. God has always intended marriage to reflect gospel realities.

My focus in this chapter is not on what's gone wrong with the world, but on what needs to go right with us—Christians. The truth of the matter is that too many of the pews across this country are filled with people whose thinking about these matters differs very little from that of the rest of the world. There has to be more to marriage than what the world alleges, and Ephesians 5:21–33 confirms that there is. God's glory is at stake in marriage and in the roles that God has assigned to husbands and wives to fulfill. Marriage is a testimony to the glory of God and the gospel itself.

God's Glory in a Wife's Submission (Eph. 5:21-24)

Paul begins with a command that applies to men and women: "Be subject to one another in the fear of Christ" (NASB). The word that Paul uses for "subject" is a military term, and it refers to ranking someone in a subordinate position. So to "be subject" to someone means to submit to their authority. But what does Paul mean by "to one another"? Some people think "to one another" means *mutual submission*—which means that everyone in the church submits to everyone. Everybody submits to everybody in the sense that we all serve one another and put one another's interests above our own. Of course we all should serve one another and put others' interests before our own, but that's not what Paul is talking about here. The word that Paul uses here is stronger than that—it's a word that denotes *authority* and *obedience* to a leader. This is what is going on in Ephesians 5. Paul isn't telling everyone to submit to everyone. He's telling one group to submit to another group.

Verse 22 explains who submits to whom in this marital relationship: "Wives, be subject to your own husbands, as to the Lord" (NASB). So Paul says that the proper authority for a wife is her own husband. But notice what he doesn't say. Paul could have said, "Husbands, subject your wives to yourselves." Paul might have spoken in such a way that called on husbands to compel or coerce submission from their wives. Such a command would have fit quite well within the patriarchal culture of Paul's day. But that's not how Paul talks. He addresses the wives and says "be subject" in the passive voice. This means that wives are called on *voluntarily* to submit to their husbands. The responsibility falls to the wives to submit themselves, not to the husbands to make them submit.

Husbands, if you ever find yourself trying to force your wife to follow your leadership, then you need to know there's a problem—especially if it is a pattern over the course of your marriage. You need to be asking yourself, *Why isn't she following me?* The answer may be that she is in rebellion against God and His role for her in marriage. That's possible. If that is the case, you can pray for her and tenderly exhort her.

But far more often, the reason she's not following is because you're being a crummy leader. When that is the case, you need to up your game as leader, but you are never to coerce or manipulate submission. Obviously, you would never physically coerce your wife to do anything, but neither can you be verbally abusive or manipulative to get your way. If you have to verbally and emotionally intimidate your wife into submission, then the problem is not her. It's you. And you need to repent.

Wives, this does mean that the onus is on you submit to your husband as to the Lord. You are not to submit to every man, just to one man—your husband. God calls you to submit to your husband "as to the Lord," which means that you should view your submission to your husband as a part of your commitment to the Lord Jesus. Wives, the narrow road that leads to life for you is the path of submission.

Paul explains why a wife should submit to her husband's leadership in verse 23: "For the husband is the head of the wife as Christ is the head of the church. He is the Savior of the body." Our culture treats leadership in marriage like it's a jump ball in basketball. The referee tosses the ball up, and whoever is bigger and stronger gets the possession. That's not how God appoints leadership in marriage. Leadership in marriage is more like an inbound pass. The referee has already assigned possession of the ball before it is thrown into play. In marriage, God has handed the ball of leadership to the husband, and he is to lead.

This verse says that the husband is the "head" of the wife—which means that he is the *authority*. Some people try to explain the husband's headship away by saying that *head* doesn't mean *authority* but *source*. But this is not what the term means. We know that because the husband's headship is patterned after Christ's headship over the church—"as Christ also is the head of the church" (NASB). And in chapter 1:22, Paul says: "And He put everything under His feet and appointed Him as head over everything for the church." Obviously, headship has to do with authority, and so in this way the husband is called to be the leader and authority in the home.

But are there limits to a wife's obligation to follow her husband's leadership? Ephesians 5:24 says, "Now as the church submits to Christ, so wives are to submit to their husbands in everything." This verse has scared a lot of people over the years. Does it really mean that a wife has to submit to her husband in everything? The analogy between Christ and husbands is not a perfect one, is it? All analogies break down if you press them too far. Christ is sinless and perfect. Husbands are not. Christ will never lead His bride into sin. We wish that the same could be said for all other husbands, but we know better. Sometimes human husbands abuse their authority. For this reason, wives are not supposed to submit to abuse or to sin. No authority on this earth is an absolute authority—not even a husband's authority. When submitting to a husband requires submitting to abuse or to sin, then the Christian wife must follow the example of Peter and the apostles in Act 5:29 who said, "We must obey God rather than men." Meaning she shouldn't submit to that.

Why then does Paul use the expansive language, "in everything"? Because God does intend for wives to orient their lives and plans around the leadership of their husbands. My wife knows my heart and vision for our home and for raising our children. Submission for her means trying to order the household around that vision even when I'm not there. There is a happy deference there that is pervasive in everything she does. That doesn't mean that it's always easy for her to do that or that I'm always right. But right or wrong, she always aims to support my leadership.

Wives, sometimes submission is difficult. And the difficulty is not always because your husband is being abusive or asking you to do something that's sinful. It may be because he's doing something that you believe to be unwise or that could be done in a better way. Oftentimes, you do actually know better than your husband. Submission for you is going to be trying to figure out how to honor your husband's leadership no matter what the situation is. You need to offer your counsel to your husband and to make sure he has all the wisdom he can glean from you as the both of you make decisions. But you also need to offer him your patience and support even when it's difficult to do so because you disagree.

God's Glory in a Husband's Love (Eph. 5:25–28)

Paul enjoins husbands to display the ultimate Christian virtue toward their wives: "Husbands, love your wives." While the wife's responsibility is to "submit," the husband's responsibility is to "love." Love in this text is not just a state of mind on the husband's part. This love issues forth in certain kinds of behaviors from the husband to the wife. We can summarize these behaviors in three words: *leadership, protection,* and *provision*. Husband, you love your wife by leading her, protecting her, and providing for her.

We've already seen the leadership assignment in verse 23, where we read that the husband is the "head of the wife." I think we see the protection and the provision implied in verses 28–29: "In the same way husbands are to love their wives as their own bodies. . . . For no one ever hates his own flesh but provides and cares for it." Men, what do you do when you are sitting at home and your stomach growls? Do you have to be talked into eating something? No. When you are hungry, you eat. You *provide* for yourself instinctively. You lead her, and you give her your protection and provision, and you do so in a way that is *instinctive*. You don't have to be told. You just do it because you're caring for her like you care for your own body.

This love is modeled on Christ's love for the church which means that it is first of all sacrificial, which is the point of verse 25: "just as Christ loved the church and gave Himself for her." Husbands, your headship in your home does not exist so that you can put your desires and needs before everyone else's. Your headship exists so that you can give yourself up for your wife like Christ gave Himself up for you. That means that being the leader, provider, and the protector is sometimes going to be hard. There are going to be times when you have a conflict with your wife. And there will be times when the conflict is her fault, and you are going to feel like disengaging emotionally from your wife. But you don't get to do that. You don't get to perform a passive aggressive sulk until your wife swallows her pride and comes to try and make amends. You are the leader. That means that you are leading the charge for reconciliation when there is a conflict. You get to treat your wife like Jesus treats you as a sinner. Did Jesus wait for you to become repentant and deserving before He drew near to you? Did Jesus lead out in your reconciliation or did you? You know the answer. Jesus did everything to win you, and you must do the same for your wife.

You might say, "But I'm really mad at her." If that is the case, then you need to put away your anger and obey Jesus. You might say, "But I'm not a real good communicator." Then you need to get better at communicating, and you need to lead your wife. You take the initiative, and you model tenderness and mercy and love and forgiveness and everything else she needs to make submitting to you a joy for her. You might say, "But that's hard!" Yes, it's hard! But Jesus blazed the trail for us, and you won't have to do anything harder than what He did to love you. So you follow Jesus and love your wife self-sacrificially.

The purpose for this kind of sacrificial love is clear: "to make her holy, cleansing her with the washing of water by the word. He did this to present to the church to Himself the church in splendor, without spot or wrinkle or anything like that, but holy and blameless" (vv. 26–27). Jesus gave Himself up for His bride with a purpose in mind for her. He wanted to sanctify her in the present and to perfect her for the last day. In other words, Jesus has His bride's total spiritual renewal in mind as He initiates reconciliation.

Husbands, does your love for your wife have a purpose? Jesus' did. Are you self-consciously calculating how you can cheer your wife on to love and good deeds? How you can encourage her to be more and more Christlike until the last day appears? If you don't have your wife's sanctification and perfection in mind, then you aren't loving her as Christ loves His bride. That is why Paul writes in verse 28: "In the same way husbands are to love their wives as their own bodies. He who loves his wife loves himself." Again, a husband's care for his wife must be instinctive and intuitive, just as he cares for himself. Because you are "one flesh" with her, her hurts, her desires, her needs, her wants, her dreams are your hurts, your desires, your needs, your wants, and your dreams.

You will never love your bride as Christ loves His bride if you are indifferent toward your spouse. Indifference and coldness can creep into a marriage after months and years and decades of passivity toward your marriage. Husbands, God has called you to *lead*, and that means that every single day you must get up and take the initiative to cultivate your vineyard (Song of Sol. 2:15). If you don't, you will wake up one day with the thistles and briars covering the face of your garden (Prov. 24:30–34). And it will be devastating to your wife, your children, and to you. And it will bring a reproach on the gospel.

God's Glory in Marriage (Eph. 5:29–33)

Verses 29–30 confirm that our marriages are to be patterned after Christ's marriage to His church: "For no one ever hates his own flesh but provides and cares for it, just as Christ does for the church, since we are members of His body." Christ provides and cares for His bride because "we are members of His body." In other words, Christ doesn't hate His own "flesh" but loves it and cares for it instinctively.

But how is it that we have become Jesus' own "flesh"? Paul explains in verse 31: "For this cause a man shall leave his father and mother, and shall cleave to his wife; and the two shall become one flesh" (NASB). This verse is a quotation of Genesis 2:24, and it is the single most important verse in all of the Bible explaining the meaning and purpose of marriage. In fact, the most important statements about marriage in the New Testament come from Jesus and Paul. And in each case, they quote the Old Testament to establish what marriage is. But when Jesus and Paul quote the Old Testament, they never point to the great polygamous kings of Israel like David or Solomon. Nor do they point to the grand polygamous patriarchs of old like Abraham or Jacob. For all their importance in biblical theology, Jesus and Paul never look to any of those figures as the paradigm for marriage. Instead, without exception, they go back to the pre-fall monogamous union of Adam and Eve in the garden, and they say, "For this cause a man shall leave his father and mother, and shall cleave to his wife; and the two shall become one flesh" (NASB). Marriage is the covenantal union before God of one man and one woman. The man and the woman leave their families to form a new family, they are united together in a conjugal bond, and they become "one flesh." *One flesh* means that they become like blood relations through the consummated covenant of marriage.

But notice that at the beginning of verse 31, Paul doesn't introduce the quotation with something like, "as it is written" or "the Scripture says." Without introduction, he just quotes the verse. Why? I think he does it because he wants that first phrase to have its real connective force, *"for this cause."* Why does a man leave his father and mother and join himself to a wife? Why does marriage exist in the world? Why is it that we have had this age-old institution that cuts across all cultures and all times and all religious groups, that one man and one woman would come together for life? Why does marriage exist? "For this cause"! "For this cause" points us back to verse 30: "Christ nourishes and cherishes His church" For that reason, marriage exists on planet Earth. Marriage exists to tell a story about Jesus' marriage to His bride.

Paul explains in verse 32: "This mystery is profound, but I am talking about Christ and the church." The key to this text is to understand the word *mystery*. When we use the word *mystery*, we are referring to something that is hidden and unknown. That's not how Paul uses this word. A mystery in Paul's vocabulary is something that was once hidden under the Old Covenant but now has been made known through the gospel (cf. Rom. 16:25–26). So when Paul says *mystery*, he's talking about something that was once hidden but has now been revealed in the gospel.

Here's the profound mystery. From the very beginning, God intended marriage to be a depiction of the gospel. *For this cause* people get married. To demonstrate to the world that Christ loves and cherishes His bride. Marriage exists to manifest the glory of Christ's redemptive love for His bride. That means that your marriage exists to display to the world the glory of Christ's redemptive love for His bride. Husbands, you are to love your bride in such a way that people can see Christ's love for His church. Wives, you are to submit to your husbands in such a way that the world can see the loveliness of Christ in the obedience of His bride. We are Christ's "flesh" and blood by covenant. We belong to our Beloved, and He belongs to us. And our marriages exist to draw attention to that reality.

Why do Jesus and Paul appeal to the first marriage to explain the meaning of all marriages? The answer has something to do with the fact that this first marriage between Adam and Eve occurred when everything was literally right with the world—before sin contaminated everything. There was no death, no strife, no pride, no lust, nor any other foxes ruining the vineyard of marriage. All was well and just as God intended it to be—one man and one woman living in perfect harmony and fellowship with God and with each other. It was the one time in human history that God could look at mankind and say that they were "good" (Gen. 1:31). It was the only time in human history when there was a perfect marriage operating according to God's creational intent. The marriage of the pre-fall Adam and Eve thus becomes the ideal for all marriages to follow.

Conclusion

So wives, do you see how God's glory is at stake in your submission? Husbands, do you see how God's glory is at stake in your love for your wife? To everyone, do you see how God's glory is at stake in our marriages?

Our witness to the world consists in large part in our marriages. We take marriage seriously because God takes it seriously.

When a marriage falls apart, it says something blasphemous about the gospel. That is why we care so much. Marriage is hard. You won't be able to do it on your own. But God can do it. God can bring to you the resources that you need to be faithful to the role that He has called you to in your marriage. But I believe you're not going to get there if you can't see the end from the beginning—if you can't see God's purpose for marriage. Marriage is not a personal lifestyle choice. Marriage is about the glory of God and about whether or not people are going to see the glory of God in the world.

Does your marriage display the gospel to the world? The Bible says that it should.

Discussion Questions

1. Why did God create marriage? What is marriage's purpose?
2. Who is the ultimate example of "headship" in Scripture? What can husbands learn from this example?
3. Are there limits to a wife's obligation to follow her husband's leadership?
4. What is the purpose of a husband's sacrificial love for his wife?
5. How is our witness to the world affected by the roles that God calls us to in marriage?

How Should the Christian Live?

Dennis Rainey

CLINT AND PENNY BRAGG MET ON THEIR CHURCH'S SOFTBALL field in 1987. Then she was part of the discipleship class he taught. Clint was impressed with Penny's commitment as a follower of Christ. "I said, 'Wow, she really is in love with the Lord. I have to get to know her after this course is over.'"

They dated for two years, then married. "It was a fairy tale come true," Clint recalls. For the next year they were pillars in their church, the golden couple. From Sunday school to worship to discipleship training to vacation Bible school, they were involved.

But something was crumbling in their relationship. Caught up in the busyness of a small church that needed lots of help, they didn't focus much on their most important relationships—with God and with each other. As Penny says, "We didn't spend a lot of time putting spiritual roots down."

A mission trip to Haiti left Penny shaken at the poverty and suffering she observed. She began to wonder why God would allow this to occur. When they returned home, with communication so poor between them, Penny began pulling away emotionally from Clint, feeling she couldn't tell him what was going on in her heart.

Clint sensed that he and Penny were becoming more isolated, but he didn't know how to fix it. Meanwhile, they kept up a façade to their church friends, acting as if they were still the golden couple.

At work, Penny began spending more and more time with a male coworker who seemed to provide the emotional support she felt she wasn't getting from Clint. Over time that friendship evolved into an affair. Clint figured out what was going on, and he gave her an ultimatum—she either needed to pack up and leave, or stay with him and do whatever it took to make the marriage work.

Penny's response was to leave and move in with her boyfriend. A few months later she and Clint were divorced.

And Clint was left feeling angry and bitter at God because he had lost the love of his life.

A Marriage Built on Shifting Sand

Have you ever been in a home with a poor foundation? It may look good on the outside, but inside you may find cracks in the walls and floor. Doors won't open or close properly. And if the foundation isn't fixed, eventually the home will begin to show problems on the exterior. Eventually the structure will fall apart.

That's what happened with Clint and Penny. Though they were followers of Christ, they lacked a solid foundation for their marriage. And eventually their relationship imploded.

Millions of couples in our country today face a similar problem. They get married to experience true oneness and partnership, but everything in life—the cultural values of independence and self-fulfillment—drives them apart. They want a fulfilling and happy relationship, but they have little idea how to make it happen. Most have never seen how a good marriage works.

Couples today just don't know what a true biblical marriage looks like. I'm reminded of the words of Jesus Christ in Matthew 7:24–27,

"Therefore, everyone who hears these words of Mine and acts on them will be like a sensible man who built his house on the rock. The rain fell, the rivers rose, and the winds blew and pounded that house. Yet it didn't collapse, because its foundation was on the rock. But everyone who hears these words of Mine and doesn't act on them will be like a foolish man who built his house on the sand. The rain fell, the rivers rose, the winds blew and pounded that house, and it collapsed. And its collapse was great!"

Note those words, "Everyone then who hears these words of mine and does them . . ." That's what wise people do—they build their lives and their home on the rock of *hearing and obeying God's Word.*

So how does this look on a day-to-day basis? How can you build your home with the right foundation? Here are some thoughts:

Learn God's Purposes for Marriage

While in Southern California on a business trip, I stopped for a red light early one morning. Waiting at the intersection, I noticed a construction crew busy renovating an old restaurant. Like ants, the carpenters and other workers were scrambling through the building, and almost every one of them possessed the same thing: blueprints.

The light turned green and I sped away, but the scene lingered in my memory, reminding me of a simple truth: You don't build or renovate a structure without blueprints. Or if you do, how will that building turn out?

Unfortunately, too many couples have not compared notes on their blueprints for marriage. Like those construction workers, every husband and every wife has a set of prints, but I've seen too many relationships where his and hers don't match—their expectations and purposes differ.

The answer for this problem is a mutual commitment to understand God's purposes and plan for marriage, which become clear in the very first book of the Bible. Marriage is central to God's plan for mankind. When a husband and wife live together in love, humility, and harmony, their relationship reflects God's image to a world that desperately needs to see who He is. As David Platt writes in his book *Counter Culture*, "When God made man, then woman, and then brought them together in a relationship called marriage . . . he was painting a picture. His intent from the start was to illustrate his love for people."[3]

Take time together to learn more about God's plan for marriage—it's far more strategic and important than you realize.

Keep Your Vows

Love isn't a feeling. Love is commitment. You can't begin a marriage without commitment, and you can't sustain one without it.

Our God is a covenant maker and keeper. God chose the covenant as His way of relating to people. The covenant is the most sacred of all pledges and promises. The first marriage covenant was achieved when God united Adam and Eve in the first wedding. Later Jesus expressed the importance of the marriage covenant when He said, "'Haven't you read,' He replied, 'that He who created them in the beginning made them male and female,' and He also said: 'For this reason a man will leave his father and mother and be joined to his wife, and the two will become one flesh? So they are no longer two, but one flesh. Therefore, what God has joined together, man must not separate'" (Matt. 19:4–6).

The covenant Jesus described was a solemn oath made by the husband and wife to each other and also to God. Many couples make such a covenant in their wedding ceremony—pledging to love each other "in sickness and in health" . . . "in poverty and in wealth" . . . "till death do us part . . . so help me God."

The problem, however, is that many modern couples consider their vows more of a contract than a covenant. A contract has an end date. A covenant is permanent, and that's how we should view marriage. In fact, I often urge couples to never use the "D-word"—divorce—in their home. Words have power. If you first think about divorce and then talk about it, before long what was once unthinkable becomes an option.

Marital commitment demands perseverance. For your sake, for the sake of your children, and for the sake of our culture, you need to remain committed to the covenant you made before God. You need to maintain the perseverance of couples like J. L. and Hilda Simpson, godly Christians who wrote me a profound note,

> *I was 15 and J. L. was 17 when we married. We are now 61 and 63. We could have divorced dozens of times but because we love each other deeply, and because God hates divorce, we didn't want to bring the curse of divorce into our family, so we didn't.*

One of the most profound ways a married couple reflects God's love is when they keep their vows and remain committed for a lifetime, no matter what they face. Doesn't God do the same with us? He never quits . . . His love is constant and everlasting . . . He never gets tired of us. That's how our commitment should look in marriage.

Deal with Your Selfishness

Frankly, many couples beginning marriage underestimate how selfishness can threaten a marriage. During courtship and engagement, we do everything we can to attract and please our loved ones. We make ourselves out to be the most kind, loving, compassionate, sensitive human beings on the earth. Then, once we are married and the conquest is complete, our natural selfishness, independence, and pride begin to bubble to the surface.

Suddenly we experience conflict, and we're shocked that this ideal love is not as pure as we imagined. Each of us wants our own way. As James 4:1–2 tells us:

> What causes quarrels and what causes fights among
> you? Is it not this, that your passions are at war
> within you? You desire and do not have, so you
> murder. You covet and cannot obtain, so you fight
> and quarrel. You do not have, because you do not
> ask. (ESV)

Marriage offers a tremendous opportunity to do something about selfishness. Someone may say, "There is no hope; I can't get him to change," or "What's the use? She'll never be any different." Barbara and I know there is hope because we learned to apply a plan that is bigger than human self-centeredness. Through principles taught in Scripture, we have learned how to set aside our selfish interests for the good of each other as well as for the profit of our marriage.

The answer for ending selfishness is found in Jesus and His teachings. He showed us that instead of wanting to be first, we must be willing to be last. Instead of wanting to be served, we must serve. Instead of trying to save our lives, we must lose them. We must love our neighbors (our spouses) as much as we love ourselves.

A marriage is built when two individuals deny their selfishness and yield to Jesus Christ for the purpose of loving and serving their spouses. Jesus Christ will begin the process of building your home if you submit to Him.

Focus on Pleasing Your Spouse (Not Yourself)

Pleasing your mate is a command of Scripture. Romans 15:1–3 reads: "Now we who are strong have an obligation to bear the weaknesses of those without strength, and not to please ourselves. Each one of us must please his neighbor for his good, to build him up. For even the Messiah did not please Himself"

Note that pleasing your spouse first requires that you not focus on pleasing yourself. God has not put us here merely to satisfy our own wants and needs. In Philippians 2:3–4, we read: "Do nothing from selfishness or empty conceit, but with humility of mind regard one another as more important than yourselves; do not merely look out for your own personal interests, but also for the interests of others" (NASB).

Romans 15:2 also exhorts us to "Each one of us must please his neighbor for his good." Who is your closest neighbor? Your spouse.

When you focus on pleasing your spouse, you are concerned for their good. You seek to help, to serve, to understand their needs.

During the early years of marriage, I remember looking in the rearview mirror of the car as I pulled out to go fishing with several of our children one Saturday. Barbara was standing on the porch, left with a couple of kids in diapers while I went off to the lake with the older kids to have a good time.

While I was sitting out in that boat, not catching anything, I continued to think about Barbara. *You know, I am pleasing myself, but I have not done a good job of pleasing her.* I realized I needed to give up some of my hobbies for a while in order to please her and reduce her burden. But you know what happened? Once the youngest kids grew older and Barbara's burden began to lift, she began to encourage me to fish and hunt with the children. When I left the house on one of these trips, I would look in the rearview mirror and see her on that same porch, waving goodbye with a smile.

Here's another area to focus on in pleasing your spouse: sex and romance. Women spell romance R-E-L-A-T-I-O-N-S-H-I-P.

Men spell romance S-E-X. If you want to speak romance to your spouse, become a student of your spouse, enroll in a life-long "Romantic Language School," and become fluent in your spouse's language.

Be Lavish in Your Forgiveness

The Scriptures have a lot to say about resolving conflict, but let me focus on just one phrase, from Colossians 3:13: "Just as the Lord has forgiven you, so you must also forgive."

Through Christ, God reached out to you and forgave you even though you were dead in your sins. He calls you to extend the same type of lavish, proactive forgiveness to those who sin against you—and especially to your spouse.

Without the cleansing power of forgiveness, at best, marriage will be very hard duty. At worst it will be disaster. No matter how much two people try to love and please each other, they will fail. With failure comes hurt. And the only ultimate relief for hurt is the soothing salve of forgiveness.

You can tell whether you have forgiven your spouse by asking yourself one question:

Have I given up my desire to punish my spouse?

When you lay aside that desire and no longer seek revenge, you free your spouse and *yourself* from the bonds of your anger.

Forgiveness cannot be conditional. Once you forgive, that's it. Feelings may still be raw, and it is not hypocritical to not feel like forgiving your spouse. If someone has hurt you, you can choose to forgive immediately but still be processing feelings of disappointment or rejection.

Forgiveness is a choice, an act of the will—not an emotion. It may take a while for your feelings to catch up with your will. But your will needs to respond to the scriptural mandate to forgive your spouse.

No question—there are some hurts, such as adulterous affairs or a spouse's addiction to pornography, that are extremely difficult to forgive and get over. There may always be some pain and distrust in the person's heart that has been so deeply offended. But we are still commanded by God to move beyond the circumstances and forgive.

That does not let the other person off the hook for completing necessary restitution and demonstrating repentance. Some boundaries may need to be erected in the relationship to prevent the sinful behavior from happening again. An intervention by a pastor, counselor, or mature friend may be required to make the sting of pain from the sin felt so sharply that the offending spouse will finally realize that the behavior has to change. No one should be allowed to continue perpetrating serious harm or a spouse.

Ultimately, though, forgiveness must rule. Anyone who says, "I cannot forgive you," really means, "I *choose* not to forgive you." If forgiveness seems impossible at that point, if prayer and reading the Scriptures do not seem to work, go to another person. Seek out a wise counselor—an elder at your church, a wise Bible teacher, a same-sex friend to confide in—and say, "Can you help me get beyond this?"

As Christians, we do not have the option of becoming embittered with our spouses. The result of obeying God and forgiving is not bondage, but freedom. Ruth Bell Graham said it well, "A good marriage is the union of two forgivers."

Live according to the 100/100 Plan

In our self-oriented culture, many couples believe that marriage should be a "50/50" relationship. The 50/50 plan basically says, "You do your part, and I'll do mine." This concept sounds logical for a marriage, but couples who use it are destined for disappointment and failure.

The big problem with this plan is that it's impossible to determine if your spouse has met you halfway. Because neither of you can agree on where halfway is, each is left to scrutinize the other's performance from a jaded, often selfish perspective.

A more biblical strategy would be the 100/100 plan, which goes like this: "I will do what I can to love you without demanding an equal amount in return." Both of you commit to giving 100 percent to the relationship, to do whatever is needed—in parenting and in housework, especially—to keep your marriage and family moving forward.

This plan is especially important during those times of sickness, or suffering, or work pressures—when one of you is unable to help like you would normally. But that's one of the wonders of marriage—to be there to help each other and lift each other up during these times of pressure and hardship.

Pray Together Every Day as a Couple

When Barbara and I were first married, I asked a man I highly respected for his best counsel on marriage. He told me that Barbara and I should pray together every day. My friend Carl said, "I've prayed every day with my Sara Jo for more than twenty-five years. Nothing has built our marriage more than our prayer time together."

We took his advice. Barbara and I usually pray together before going to sleep, but there have been some nights over the years when neither one of us felt like praying. The Lord has gently reminded me, "You need to pray with her." And even though on occasion I've not even wanted to talk to her, I have finally rolled over and said, "Let's pray." Our obedience to this spiritual discipline has reminded us of who really is the Source of strength in our marriage and has kept us connected and communicating.

Build a Relationship That Will Outlast Your Parenting Years

How long has it been since you spent extended, focused time with your spouse? Not just an evening at a fantastic eatery, but a couple of days away from your usual environment to catch up with each other? In too many marriages, the demands of the ordinary grind seem to overwhelm the possibility of extraordinary excitement.

Because of our fast-paced culture, we need to pause once or twice a year to rest, count our blessings, and dream some dreams. When our kids were still at home, Barbara and I would regularly take what we called planning weekends, an opportunity to evaluate our marriage and parenting and, if necessary, redirect plans.

Even though our kids are grown now, we still make it a point to get away for weekends and vacations together on a regular basis. The getaway is effective in keeping our communication current, and it's just plain fun. Without any of the everyday distractions, we can concentrate on romancing each other. I can give Barbara flowers and speak tender words. She can give me undivided attention as I unwind and share from the heart. We can stay up munching snacks, listening to music or talking, and we don't have to get up in the morning to meet a demanding schedule.

Fulfill Your Unique Roles and Responsibilities

During the last few decades, our culture has redefined the meaning and responsibilities of men and women in society and in the home. These social changes have led to such confusion that the very idea of gender "roles" in a marriage feels repugnant and "outdated" to many people.

But when you read passages such as 1 Corinthians 11:3 and Ephesians 5:22–30, it becomes clear that God has devised a set of responsibilities for husbands and wives, and that these roles are more profound than many of us realize. Ephesians 5:23–24 tells us, "The husband is the head of the wife as Christ is the head of the church. He is the Savior of the body. Now as the church submits to Christ, so wives are to submit to their husbands in everything."

Pastor and author David Platt writes of this passage,

> In other words, God designs husbands to be a reflection of Christ's love for the church in the way they relate to their wives, and God designs wives to be a reflection of the church's love for Christ in the way they relate to their husbands.

But talk about countercultural! Or maybe more aptly put, talk about politically incorrect! *The husband is the head of his wife? Wives should submit to their husbands? Are you serious?*[4]

One problem we face in understanding this passage today is that for centuries these truths have been misused and abused. For example, rather than adopting the biblical role of a servant/leader who models his leadership on that of Christ, many husbands have used their power and position to dominate and control their wives.

But when correctly interpreted and applied, these concepts not only result in freedom for the husband and wife, but also help you work better as a team to combat isolation and conflict in your marriage. For many Christian couples, a true biblical understanding of roles and responsibilities is critical to revitalizing their relationship.

Rely on God during Times of Hardship and Suffering

As you make God the center of your home, and commit together to obeying Scripture, the foundation of your home will grow strong and solid. And that will help you prepare for the storms of life—particularly the inevitable difficulties you will face together. In fact, when I hear of couples who buckle under the storms of life, my suspicion is they have not put down a firm foundation for their home.

Barbara and I have weathered numerous times of hardship, and we have discovered that, as we make God and His Word the focus of our relationship and home, the trials and tribulations strengthen rather than weaken our relationship. Most important, we use the suffering as an opportunity to draw close to God. After all, nothing happens in our lives apart from what He allows or ordains. As 1 Chronicles 29:11 tells us, "Yours, LORD, is the greatness and the power and the glory and the splendor and the majesty, for everything in the heavens and on earth belongs to You. Yours, LORD, is the kingdom, and You are exalted as head over all."

This same sovereign Lord also seeks a close relationship with us. He is our Comforter during times of distress and suffering. Psalm 34:18 reminds us, "The LORD is near the brokenhearted; He saves those crushed in spirit."

As a team we work together to hold fast to the truth of God's Word and to keep our marriage a priority. We need our foundation to stay strong.

Develop a Common Mission

If you are serious about glorifying God in your marriage and representing God to a fallen world, you will view your children and your friends and neighbors in a different light.

God's original plan called for the home to be a sort of greenhouse—a nurturing place where children grow up to learn character, values, and integrity. Your responsibility as a couple is to make your home a place where your children learn what it means to love and obey God. Your home should be a training center to equip your children to look at the needs of people and the world through the eyes of Jesus Christ. If children do not embrace this spiritual mission as they grow up, they may live their entire lives without experiencing the privilege of God using them in a significant way.

I also encourage you to recognize the opportunities you have beyond your immediate family. Wherever you live, there are people who are desperate to know God and to experience marriage as He designed it. A strong, committed marriage is a beacon of hope in our culture—now more than ever. Get involved in your church and community in helping people know Christ, and use your home as a gathering place where people are nourished and trained just as your children are.

Conclusion

These are just some of the steps to building a solid foundation for your marriage. All have a common thread—a relationship with God and obedience to His Word. Christ needs to be the head of your home.

That's what Clint and Penny Bragg, the couple I described at the beginning of this chapter, learned in the years after their divorce. Through different circumstances, each came to a point where they realized that living life in their own power was not working. Facing tremendous financial pressure, Clint realized he had not been walking with God. He admitted his anger—that he had blamed God for the divorce. He admitted his own fault in the marriage. "Lord, I am turning everything over to You. Do whatever You need to do."

Penny reached a similar turning point nine years after the divorce. She felt God's Spirit leading her to reconcile relationships she had broken with family and friends, but saved Clint to the end because she feared how he would react. They hadn't communicated in eleven years, but she tracked him down, and one day Clint arrived home to find a letter from Penny Bronzini—her maiden name—in his mailbox.

He sat and looked at the letter. "God, should I open this or not? Is this bad news? She's the love of my life. What does she want now?"

In the letter Penny told him what was happening in her life. She asked for his forgiveness and asked him to write or call. That night they talked for five hours—what they now call "The Grand Conversation."

Clint told Penny, "Didn't you know I forgave you a long time ago?"

"How could you?" she replied. "I never asked."

"Because Jesus forgave me. I learned that during our time apart—the depth of my sin on the cross, that Christ forgave me. So, also, should I forgive you."

Six months later—in August of 2002—Clint and Penny Bragg remarried, and since then they've been building their marriage on a solid foundation. They learned about building spiritual and emotional intimacy, about humility, about their roles. And they now work full-time helping couples understand what God can do in their marriage. No matter how dark their lives are, they tell couples, God will forgive and restore them.

Your marriage is far more important than you may have ever imagined because it affects God's reputation on this planet. That's why it's essential for you to set Jesus Christ apart as the builder of your home.

Discussion Questions

· · · · · · · · · · · · · · · · · ·

1. How can Jesus' teaching about building strong foundations (Matt. 7:24–27) be applied to marriage? Why is it important to build a strong foundation, and what are some practical ways to do this?

2. Why is it important to use a blueprint when constructing a building? How does this apply to the purposes and expectations encountered in marriage? How can

Christian couples make sure they are working from the same blueprint?

3. Why is it important to understand marriage as a covenant rather than a contract? What are the biblical expectations for entering a covenant, and how is this instructive for understanding marriage?

4. Sometimes it can be difficult to "give up the desire to punish my spouse." Why is it important to cultivate forgiveness in marriage, and how can the forgiveness offered by Christ serve as a model?

5. The steps presented in this chapter share a common thread—a relationship with God and a commitment to obey His Word. How does a committed marriage represent Christ's relationship to His church, and how can this relationship help us fulfill the unique roles and responsibilities in our own marriages?

How Should the Church Engage?

Dean Inserra

"CAN WE GET TOGETHER FOR LUNCH THIS WEEK?"

As a pastor, this is a question I am asked often, many times by people who want to discuss their relationship woes or air grievances about a recent decision made by church leadership. In this instance, a church member asked me, and I agreed to get together for a lunch meeting, not knowing what to expect. We sat down and made small talk, analyzing the football game from the night before, and shortly after our brisket and cheese grits arrived, my lunch friend got to the reason for our meeting.

"What's the most important decision one can ever make in life?"

Before I had time to answer, he pressed in.

"What would you say?" he asked aggressively.

I was relieved to receive such a "softball question" from another believer. This one was easy. I gave a solid gospel answer that would have made my seminary professors proud. I explained that how one responds to the good news of what Jesus has done for sinners, what we call "the gospel," is the most important decision any person can and will ever make. I gave a brief overview of what it means to repent and believe the gospel and took a sip of my sweet tea, feeling like my answer would satisfy this man's need to talk a little theology with his pastor.

I tried moving the conversation back to football and was ready to wrap up our meeting, but he clearly wanted more than my go-to gospel answer. He asked me to award a silver medal in life decisions, wanting my opinion on the second most important decision one could ever make in life. Maybe I was tired from watching the game the night before, or perhaps I hadn't given this question enough thought. My pause seemed to drag on to him as he waited for my answer. Again, he didn't seem to have time to wait for my answer to come.

"Who you marry! That's the second most important decision you ever make, after believing the gospel," he answered passionately for me.

I was now embarrassed over the amount of people in the restaurant staring at us, convinced that even the cooks in the kitchen had heard him. Instantly a, "Well, of course," response popped into my mind. His runner-up for the most important decision in life was spot-on, not even close. Had we wanted to go further, identifying a third place might have taken longer to debate than two youth pastors discussing Calvinism and Arminianism at Waffle House till 3:00 a.m., but second place was crystal clear—who one chooses to marry is important.

I simply replied to my lunch buddy, "You're right, that is it without a doubt."

His words that followed quickly revealed why he wanted to get together. He wanted to challenge me as his pastor to focus on what truly matters most.

"You are consistent and faithful at proclaiming the decision that is most important," he encouraged me. "Every week the gospel is made crystal clear in a way that ministers to the church member and the guest. However, besides a relationships sermon series every year, we don't spend enough time focusing on marriage. Many in our congregation have already made this decision and need the frequent biblical assurance of the implications of their decisions, and the rest will likely make that decision one day. I cannot think of a more important area of discipleship for a local church than to make marriage an ultimate priority."

I don't want to state one of the overused claims in our culture that this conversation "changed my life," but it absolutely impacted my ministry, and the church where I pastor. If choosing a spouse is the second most important decision one will ever make, marriage must be at the centerpiece of the conversation for the local church; and a culture of marriage should exist throughout the congregation.

Theology, Marriage, and the Local Church

The local church must have a culture of marriage, for theological reasons.

Practically, the significance of choosing whom to marry and the implications of that decision following nuptials is certainly a reason for the local church to make marriage an area of prime concern. It is not, however, the chief reason. The local church must take marriage seriously first and foremost for theological reasons. Marriage should have the attention of the church because it is the prerogative of God. One simple page turn in Genesis describes God's glorious design for His signature creation, the human race. The first created human beings, named Adam and Eve, were distinctly designed as male and female, made by God to provide companionship and complement one another, since it was "not good for the man to be alone." These distinct yet complementary persons were designed, customized, and crafted exclusively for each other. In celebration of finding the one designed for him, "And the man said: This one, at last, is bone of my bone and flesh of my flesh; this one will be called 'woman,' for she was taken from man" (Gen. 2:23).

This God-ordained union would be the very means by which the earth would be populated with the image bearers of God. Adam and Eve were given the mandate to multiply by having children through the act of becoming one flesh intimately, through sexual intercourse, enjoying one another without shame while participating in God' grand composition of marriage. The glory of God was on display and His divine blueprint for the expansion of humanity through companionship flourished.

As we continue reading through Genesis, the description of events quickly introduces the entrance of sin into the world as willful rebellion against God's reign. Of greatest consequence, sin separated man from God and also deeply affected the marriage relationship. For the first time, innocence was lost and the man and woman experienced shame in their nakedness. The now sinful man and woman would be banned from the presence of God.

Yet the divine plan for marriage was just beginning, as the tempting serpent would one day be struck by one who would come from a woman. Mary would give birth to the Son of God, Jesus Christ. He came from heaven and lived a sinless life, died on the cross, bearing the full penalty of the sins. Three days after His death He rose from the dead so that all who would repent and have faith in Him would see their relationship with God restored, and the effects from the sins of the first man and woman reversed.

This Good News known as the gospel is God's message of reconciliation for His created people, the church, and is to be proclaimed and understood throughout creation. In His sovereign design, the visible portrait of this gospel is found in the cornerstone of marriage, the one-flesh union between a man and a woman as husband and wife.

The one flesh that is achieved is no less than sexual intercourse, but is truly more. The marriage of Adam and Eve foreshadowed the great marriage to come between Christ and His bride, the church. When God created them male and female, He had the gospel in mind, giving the world a visible picture, of the supernatural reality of the union between Christ and the church. The one-flesh marriage union ultimately points to being one with Christ. God has given us marriage. This is His "Plan A" for the flourishing and multiplying of the human race, and His basis for a visible picture of the marriage between Christ and the church.

Culture, Marriage, and the Local Church

The local church must have a culture of marriage for cultural reasons.

While the local church must be champions and advocates for marriage because of theological and practical reasons, the church must also be aware of the importance of articulating marriage for cultural reasons. While God has given us marriage as the cornerstone of society, culture has declared marriage a capstone, a milestone we reach eventually and tack on to the rest of our lives. This view of marriage has infiltrated the local church, where twenty-first-century believers often practically and functionally agree with the world's view of marriage.

God created a man and a woman and brought them together to be husband and wife. This was to be the "once and for all" human relationship by which one would build a life. If we fast-forward to the twenty-first century, marriage is now viewed as an eventual milestone one reaches after first "experiencing life." Pursue a Master's degree, travel Europe, have a large sum of money in savings, and then once it is finally time to settle down, start to think about getting married. Marriage, if an option at all, is to be pursued after the plan of one's ambitions and dreams has been established. God, however, gave us marriage. The local church must have the courage to speak against this "capstone" worldview.

In a world where couples living together before marriage is the norm, this begins with challenging the local church's own members. A traditional practice in American culture is for the man who desires to get engaged to his girlfriend to ask the woman's father for her hand in marriage. Frequently, the immediate response from the father, after the nervous boyfriend formally asks for permission, is to ask how this young man plans to support his daughter. With this question, the father is often exclusively referring to a financial plan. This traditional American question is the practice of many unbelievers and believers alike. It has become a type of pastime or tradition, a milestone in the process of getting married. On the surface this is not an inappropriate question, as it is hardly unreasonable for a father to make sure his daughter is going to have a husband who plans on providing for his family. It does, however, point to a larger issue that assists in producing the modern-day approach to marriage as something you build toward, rather than what you build from.

The biblical view of marriage as a cornerstone sets this criteria: A Christian marrying another Christian of the opposite sex, remaining faithful to one's spouse, and committing to one another for as long as you both shall live. Personally, I will always be grateful to my father-in-law for not asking me the traditional question about financial provision. My now-wife and I were getting ready to graduate from college and desired to be married before I moved states away to attend seminary. If her father would have asked me my plans to provide for his daughter, I would have looked at him with nothing but a frozen stare, having no idea. Our plan was to get engaged, get married, move away to seminary and figure out the rest when we got there. If marriage for us had been something to build toward, I would have either needed a prolonged engagement to save money, or to postpone seminary so I could have a full-time job and provide a middle class income at best for my wife. For us, marriage was something we desired to build our lives from. We wanted to figure out our future together, as husband and wife, participating in God's cornerstone relationship for the human race.

A prolonged dating or engaged season would have also increased our sexual temptation, as a man and woman who were very attracted to each other. What a tragedy when Christians view financial instability, or pursuing "bucket-list" ambitions, as more significant than sexual immorality. We should expect this from the world, not from the local church. Pastors must challenge a capstone mind-set from the pulpit and through conversations in coffee shops, creating a church culture that sees marriage as something God gave us, not something you settle into once you've had a chance to experience life.

The church must point dating Christian couples to marriage. If a dating relationship doesn't have a plan and has no intention to head to the wedding altar, it needs to proceed very cautiously, or be dissolved altogether, rather than waste the time, emotions, and affections on something temporary. God gave us marriage to be a permanent covenant.

Holiness, Marriage, and the Local Church

The church must have a culture of marriage for the sake of holiness.

If there is an area of life that lacks enough distinction between Christians and non-Christians, I believe it is in the aspects of the relational category we call "exclusive dating." By dating, I don't mean the casual night out where you get to know someone of the opposite sex, but the exclusive serious relationships that individuals usually engage in with several different people in their lives before they get married. Prior to the sexual revolution, a man would pursue a woman toward marriage. Nowadays a man pursues a woman to be in a dating relationship. This is not necessarily a bad thing. It just makes life quite complicated for the Christian who is trying to live in holiness, because the category of dating is something we culturally invented, whereas holiness comes from God. When a concept is created by culture, so are the rules for living out that concept.

The Bible does not acknowledge dating, a category of relationships so central to our society. Boyfriends and girlfriends and being "committed" to someone who is not your spouse are all foreign to God's design. Paul wrote that we look like people "who don't know God" (1 Thess. 4:5) when we are in sexual sin. Dating makes this complicated and is now so much a part of our culture and a modern-day prerequisite for engagement that the local church must know how to approach this in Christian discipleship. The answer is not to try and overhaul a central component of our society, but rather to understand that following Jesus actually will interfere with our lives in the area of dating relationships and cause us to approach these relationships differently than unbelievers.

Again, as Paul said to the Thessalonians, we should not act like those who do not know God. A crucial first step in dating wisely and in a way that moves toward holiness is for couples to stop acting like they're married when they are not. We often treat these dating relationships as though they are quasi-marriages, ascribing to them a measure of security that God never intended and that doesn't actually exist. In dating, there is the experience of the delight of a marriage covenant, without the demands. Should the believer really be giving oneself away emotionally, romantically, and sexually to someone who is not his or her husband or wife? Exclusive emotional and physical dating relationships that are not on the path toward marriage are foreign to the Christian understanding of male and female relationships. This may even happen several times throughout one's life with different people. Heavy kissing, saying, "I love you" in a non-neighborly way, is not what we find in the Scriptures for the unmarried. I just can't see how we can make the case that should happen with multiple partners in a lifetime, as Christians, when God gave us marriage.

Foreplay Is Not in Play

There is one purpose and one purpose only for what known as "foreplay." The purpose is that it prepares you for an leads you to sex. It was not designed to stop before a clima It is absolutely what the Scriptures would designate as "sexu immorality." A church that is truly committed to the disciple ship of men and the protection of women will get serious abor sexual sin. Foreplay, nakedness, and sex are not for dating peopl in-love people, or mature people, but for married people. Fleein sexual immorality should become normal, not radical.

When the church won't discuss sexual sin, they shouldn expect others to take it seriously either. What is emphasize from the pulpit will influence the hearts of the congregatio The church should discourage extended periods of engagemen as the temptation of sexual immorality will only be heightene and the faux marriage more extensively practiced. "Wisdom" an "boundaries" should be normal words used in discussions abor dating. Holiness is the goal for those who are living to worsh God in response to the gospel of Jesus Christ. Christian datir relationships should look different, because God gave us marriag

Conclusion

Christians are called to recover and pursue God's design fo human sexuality, which is that "Both the man and his wife we naked, yet felt no shame" (Gen. 2:25). This only exists in marriage. Our communities are rampant with pornography, available wherever and whenever one desires. Adultery and divorce wreck families and create broken homes across the city. A college student wakes up with a pregnancy scare, and calling Planned Parenthood is the first thing that crosses her mind. Same-sex marriage is the new normal, and your child comes home from school asking why a classmate "has two mommies and no daddy."

We cannot minister in our cities as we want them to be, but rather as they actually are, broken and in need of the gospel of Jesus Christ.

My aforementioned lunch conversation centered on a church member who believed, for all practical purposes, the church needed to talk about marriage. He had a good point; we do need to talk about marriage more. However, the stakes are much higher than people making a big decision of exchanging vows and rings. The further one drifts away from what God has given us, the more broken he becomes. Our love of neighbor should not let us tolerate such a state of affairs. The church does not need to give more pointers on how to have a great marriage. While there is certainly a place for those helpful tips, we must assume the mission of search and rescue, pursue and recover, for the sake of our neighbors who need to be restored to God's grand design. He has given us marriage, the only place under His gospel where one can be naked and unashamed. The local church must proclaim this from the rooftops and model it for the sake of our cities, and for the sake of the world.

Discussion Questions

1. What are some additional ways in which marriage and dating, as they are commonly practiced today, distort God's design?

2. Has an understanding of the biblical ideal of marriage been lost in the evangelical church? Why or why not?

3. Based on Scripture, how would you counsel a Christian dating couple who is acting like a married couple for all intents and purposes?

4. In what ways, if any, do modern dating practices mirror how people approach their relationship with Christ and the church?

5. The church is described as the "bride of Christ." Based on this parallel, what are three things that are true of the Christ-church relationship that should be true of marriages?

5

What Does the Culture Say?

Andrew T. Walker

IN JANUARY 2015, MEDIA OUTLETS BROKE THE NEWS THAT author Nicholas Sparks and his wife were separating.

You might recall who Nicholas Sparks is. He's the author of numerous romance novels, many of which have been turned into popular movies. Movies such as *The Notebook* depict idealized portraits of unrequited love finding eventual fulfillment. As each story goes, each concludes with a "Happily Ever After" type story where the couple sails off to marital bliss. But it's not all just sappy love stories. Sparks also nobly portrays the beauty of marriages that last long into the decades where, eventually, one spouse is by the other as he or she passes away.

But, there's no small amount of irony to the story that the marriage of America's premier romance novelist broke down. The picture of marriage so masterfully told by Sparks apparently could not be attained in his own life.

If anybody should have mastered the art of romance and marriage, surely, it would have been Nicholas Sparks. How could it happen? How could America's best romance novelist have a failed marriage?

I don't know what led to their divorce; and I don't mean to celebrate, blame, or make Sparks somehow more hypocritical than others when their marriages fail, but I do want to use the example of Sparks to communicate a profound truth about marriage that we're not being told: *The truth about marriage is a lot harder—not just stranger—than the fiction we're often told by the culture.*

Marriage is hard work, and this fact is often paved over or overlooked in popular portrayals of marriage in our culture and many times evidenced in the reasons we marry at all. Hollywood doesn't help much, either. From the looks of it, Hollywood is one of the greatest ironies in today's marriage culture.

Hollywood stories sentimentalize marriage, depicting marriage as an effortless pursuit of the protagonist's strongest natural impulses. Beautiful people enjoying the lives and bodies of other beautiful people, forever and ever—isn't that the way marriage works in your family tree? I doubt it.

And then, Hollywood people glamorize marriage as the climaxing fulfillment of long, sought-after love. Every movie, it seems, ends with a relationship heading toward the altar. Yet, when we look at the *actual* celebrity marriages coming out of Hollywood, we see a different picture of marriage than the one we see depicted at the movie theater. How often do we hear of celebrity marriages falling apart? Almost weekly, tabloids report about the latest Hollywood breakup. I remember seeing one entertainment website that asked Hollywood couples who had been married for ten years what the secret was to the longevity of their marriage. It assumed that ten years by Hollywood standards was the real-world equivalent of sixty years. Ten years?

In the conversation that our culture has given us on marriage, we've consumed a lot of problematic, contradictory thinking. The institution that the majority of us want to enter, and which most of assume to be vital for both personal and public reasons, is one of the institutions most fraught with problems. Think about it: How on earth did we get to a place where the contract between you and your plumber has more legal safeguards and obligations than your marriage?

Mistaken Assumptions about Marriage

Marriage isn't just about you or your happiness. It isn't just about the bond you forge with your spouse. As the other authors make clear in this book, marriage is an institution ordained by God given to humanity to prosper it.

As the story is often told in America, those whose marriages are most romantic, or those whose marriages which are the happiest, are the marriages that survive. Why is this? To answer, we have to see that today's culture largely views marriage through an emotional, personal, or sentimental lens. Marriage, we're told, is about a couple's happiness.

There's a word for this: *saccharine*. That's a big word, I know. But it means excessively sentimental. It's the gushy, over-the-top portrayal of marriage that sees the whole enterprise of marriage as based on the emotional or sexual fulfillment of the couple. This is the dominant view of today's view on marriage.

The media is caught up with shows like *The Bachelor* that aspire to see on-air romance begin between handsome bachelors and a parade of stunningly beautiful women. If only marriage was that easy; if only marriage was about identifying the positive factors that make companionship possible. But marriage is about a lot more than that, which is what the chapters in this book all argue for.

As I've written elsewhere, marriage is the greatest "unexamined assumption" of our time.[5] It is an institution that almost everyone universally aspires to enter. This is why from the youngest of ages young girls begin idealizing what their future wedding day will look like. They know that there is something powerful in the portrait of a woman in a flowing white dress with cascading adornments gracefully walking down the aisle where "the man of her dreams" awaits her. There are also ironies built into our marriage culture. Consider this astonishing statistic: According to costofwedding.com, the average wedding costs $26,444 in America. Yet, this emphasis on the event—the wedding—often eclipses the point of the event—the marriage. Americans invest so much energy preparing for weddings and so little in preparing for actual marriages.

But the messages of mass media and culture haven't translated into the experience of how marriage is fairing as an institution in American culture. What's driving this new understanding of marriage, one that sees emotional and erotic ecstasy as the main reason for entering marriage? Before looking at particular causes that drive or shape our understanding of marriage today, it's important to remember that the reason most things happen in culture can rarely be traced back to a single source. Usually, there are numerous forces at work that create a perfect storm to help shape or bend our understanding of something in culture.

Understanding How Culture Can Affect Marriage

Marriage has undergone several redefinitions and is now in a state of free fall.

Consider these sobering realities:

- Marriage rates are at an all-time low. This means that fewer and fewer people are marrying.[6]
- Young Americans are marrying later in life than ever before.[7]
- Younger Americans are having more children outside of marriage than ever before.[8]
- Living together, or what's called "cohabitation," is in many cases replacing marriage, provoking one news outlet to call it "the new normal."[9]
- Experts believe that between 40 to 50 percent of all marriages now end in divorce.[10]
- Same-sex marriage is now legal in all fifty states.

What happened in the culture that caused this set of statistics to be possible?

Marriage has undergone a profound transformation. Once understood as a *covenant*, marriage today is now thought of more as a *contract*. A covenant is a bond that is sealed by an oath or vow. It promises mutual obligation and permanence. A covenant is something assumed to be enduring. A contract, on the other hand, is easier to break. Parties can walk away from a contract based on set, mutually agreed upon terms. If the terms are broken, one party walks away. That's not the case with a covenant.

We saw this profound transformation occur with the sexual revolution. The sexual revolution was—like the words sound, a revolution—about sexuality and morality that took place in the 1960s and 1970s. A product of many factors such as greater economic opportunity, youth rebellion, and the introduction of mass-produced contraception, Americans for the first time became more sexually free or sexually expressive. Advocates for sexual freedom thought that they were empowering individuals to experience the essence of freedom: personal autonomy. Out with the old moral order of sexual repression and in with the new moral order of sexual celebration, so we were told.

Culture and Marriage Redefined

We can't understand our culture's definition of marriage today without first understanding the redefinition that occurred in the past. Indeed, we are simply the recipients of a culture that began long ago.

In general, a *redefinition* occurs when something's essence or nature has been altered, added to, or subtracted from. What does *redefinition* mean as applied to marriage? In the case of marriage, a redefinition occurs when the goods of marriage are removed from the marriage itself and experienced elsewhere in a

substitute and cheapened form. A "good" is a feature that is goo
for its own sake and stands on its own. This will be explaine
shortly. Once the goods of marriage are capable of being attaine
apart from marriage, the need to enter marriage to experienc
those goods and benefits becomes less necessary. For the sak
of this chapter's argument, let us assume that marriage's good
are threefold: romantic union, companionship, and procreatio
Once these goods were de-coupled from the bounds of marriag
the likelihood of marriage's further devaluation and redefinitio
were inevitable.

Sex without Marriage?

Starting in the 1950s and 1960s with the introduction
industrialized access to hormonal contraception, America bega
its sexual revolution. For the first time in American culture, se
ual intercourse could be experienced recreationally. As a resul
sexual activity as something not necessarily marital became a
increased reality. Now, it would be both ignorant and naïve
assume that up until this era people who were not married we
somehow all sexually abstinent. This surely was not the cas
Rather, what occurred starting in the 1950s and 1960s was th
idea that sex need not occur strictly within the boundaries
marriage. Over time, social taboos around promiscuity lessene
such that the formerly sacred assumption that sex be reserved f
marriage is now itself a taboo. Whether one calls it "pre-marit

sex" or "fornication," the idea that sex was an activity reserved only for spouses became outdated.

No longer was the marital act—what Scripture calls the one-flesh union (Gen. 2:24)—believed to belong exclusively within the confines of marriage. Once sex is removed from marriage where it was designed to occur, marriage—and what happens inside it—becomes redefined. This notion of intercourse being inherently conjugal (as related to a husband and wife) is echoed in the apostle Paul's admonition in 1 Corinthians 6:18 to flee sexual immorality. According to Paul's logic, to sexually join one's self to an individual not your spouse is to engage in an act reserved for marriage. To this line of thinking, a sexual act is a marital act.

Thus, once sexual intimacy is severed from marital intimacy, a redefinition of marriage and what it is reserved for has taken place.

Sex without Babies?

The act that seals or bonds the marriage union is the same act that brings forth life. Through the sexual union of a husband and wife, the potential for children and the common task of caring and providing for any children, are united. Though contraceptive devices vary, and indeed, while some forms are more morally problematic than others, contraception by its very nature acts to disrupt what would otherwise be the logical purpose of sexual intercourse—new life. The impact of contraception forged a new paradigm of sexual activity: childless sex. Once the effects of sex can be cut off from the premises of sex, it would not take long until sexual activity would be misused (and at no small harm to women and children as a result).

Now, as a Protestant Christian, I do not personally hold to a prohibitionist position concerning contraception. My concerns with contraception are its effects in introducing and radicalizing sexual autonomy in general and the after-effects of de-linking children altogether from the sexual bond.

Coupling the assumption that sex is (wrongly) no longer reserved for the marital union with the introduction of childless sex, yet another redefinition of marriage has taken place. Once the idea is introduced that sex must no longer allow for children, one will see how overstating contraception's contribution to marriage's redefinition cannot be emphasized too strongly.

Once sexual intimacy is severed from procreation, a redefinition of marriage and its connection to family life has taken place.

Marriage and Cohabitation

In recent years, the practice of living together prior to marriage, or in place of marriage altogether, has become routine and often assumed as standard practice amongst the young adult population. Its popularity is widespread and considered yet another step in the path toward relationship success.

The phenomenon communicates something very clearly: deep, lifelong commitment that only marriage was once believed to offer individuals is now available through a pseudo-form of marriage known as "living together" or, more technically, cohabitation. Singles unsure of whether their potential mate meets all of the criteria, so they think, utilize the practice to test-drive what they're eyeing as a long-term investment. This is, of course, silly, and cheapens marriage by reducing it to a pre-nuptial agreement based on preferences of whether and how badly their potential spouse impedes on their idea of a perfect spouse. Foregoing living together refines those who commit to make their marriage work, regardless of whatever unpleasant habits one spouse discovers in another.

Once sexual intimacy and lifelong companionship are severed from either a legal or covenantal marker, a redefinition of marriage and its connection to companionship and fidelity has taken place.

Marriage and Divorce

Prior to the 1970s, one party had to admit fault in order to obtain a legal divorce. Whether adultery, abuse, or abandonment, simply walking away from a marriage out of inconvenience was not a reality allowable by law.

While obtaining a divorce was always a legal possibility prior to No-Fault Divorce (NFD) laws, the law upheld marriage as an institution assumed permanent and divorce as an exception. While hard to pinpoint a definite correlation and causation relationship, one would have to think that it is not by coincidence that No-Fault Divorce arrived on the American landscape right around the time of hormonal contraception. The de-linking of sex from childbearing, the opportunity at recreational and non-committal sex, and the easy dissolution of soured marriages work together too strongly to simply be accidental.

Today, no phenomenon has helped to calcify and atrophy marriage and cause relationship burnout more than the prevalence and availability of divorce, and not without enormous social costs in its wake. From economic hardship brought on by single parenting to the emotional turmoil by those involved in severed marriage, divorce has fundamentally altered the family make-up of the American experience.

If marriage is no longer a bedrock of permanence, the possibility of its dissolution and abandonment amounts to redefinition.

Marriage and Its Imitators

We now find ourselves at what seems like the culmination of marriage's redefinition: same-sex marriage. How did we arrive at this point in time where two persons of the same-sex are eligible for marriage? Because, once again, the goods of marriage that are so enticing and inherent to marriage are now assumed widely available apart from the conjugal union of a husband and wife. Once the connection between marriage and family life is severed; once sex is believed to function without children; once companionship is esteemed and valued apart from marriage, it is only logical that the gay community will desire to imitate what natural marriage once exclusively offered. Thus, arriving where we have at this stage, it should be no surprise that once the goods of marriage have collapsed beneath the weight of heterosexual revision, attempts by gay persons to experience not only the goods of marriage, but the essence of marriage, will occur as well.

But same-sex marriage has its own problems. The logic of same-sex marriage presents no principle in itself that won't further chip away at marriage's design. Think about this: If two same-sex persons can marry, why must marriage be considered permanent or exclusive? If you remove the male-female component of marriage, the very idea of marriage falls apart. Those of us engaged in the debate about family structure in America have been predicting this for some time, often to the laughs and jeers of our opponents. But if any principle can stand true amidst the sexual revolution, it is this: give it enough time, and anything is possible.

As I have said, marriage is in a state of free fall in America. It's been subject to numerous definitions that are proving that the move to "expand" the eligibility of who can marry isn't drawing people's interest in marriage; rather, it is defining marriage down. Where's the proof? Proof is in the terminology that o[…] Brave New World is concocting concerning marriage and huma[…] sexuality. Words like:

- *Throuple:* Similar to "couple," the concept of a "throupl[…] was profiled in *New York Magazine* profiling a thre[…] person couple.

- *Wedlease:* The idea promoted by a lawyer in t[…] *Washington Post* who suggested that marriage shou[…] be term-limited. If the marriage is successful after, f[…] example, five years, the couple could renew their ma[…] riage for another term.

- *Monogamish:* As opposed to monogamy that restric[…] sexuality to only those in the marriage, this new conce[…] has been championed by sex columnist Dan Savage wh[…] suggested that marital infidelity is okay so long as ea[…] partner is open and honest about their infidelity.[11]

- *Conscious uncoupling:* This phrase was used by celebri[…] Gwyneth Paltrow when she announced that she and h[…] husband—though divorcing—were really undergoing[…] "conscious uncoupling" that refuses to see their divor[…] in negative terms.[12]

Conclusion

A while back, *Vanity Fair* magazine did a lengthy profile on the dating app "Tinder."[13] This app allows users to quickly identify other users in their area who find one another attractive. Rather than being an online dating site, it has devolved into a "hook-up" app that helps users quickly identify and message other users who are looking for quick sex. The article is a devastating portrait of the after-effects and consequences of marriage's erosion in America.

In it, the author interviews both male and female users of Tinder, who all attest to the sexual excess that Tinder enables. Female users complain of feeling cheapened and objectified by men whose promiscuity now had endless outlets. Male users talk of women they've had sex with as someone would talk about playing a game of pick-up basketball: casual, fun, and no-strings-attached.

But the article really points out the silent screams and heartache brought on by the sexual revolution and the collapse of marriage in today's culture. Longing for deep intimacy, women are seen as objects to conquer, rather than as delicate counterparts to be loved and pursued. Men are reduced to the very worst of male sexuality—seen as primitive hunters looking to copulate as much and as often as will be allowed.

The article screams heartache as rising generations are increasingly unable to form deep relationships.

How should Christians think through this, not just Tinder, but the larger reality that Americans are over-sexed, but relationship-starved? How else do we make sense of the new phenomenon where professional services offer the opportunity to "cuddle" with someone non-sexually?[14]

The article is soaked with despair, irony, and unfulfillment. We think we know what satisfies, but we don't. Because the human appetite craves novelty, we're led to believe by fallen desires that indulging in as much consensual, non-monogamous sex as possible, we will enrich our lives. That is demonstrably false, both biblically, and from the online testimony of both men and women who are now ritually unable to have lasting relationships because "hooking up" has displaced the role of real, lasting, and deep intimacy. The negative effects and outcomes that the article profiles—psychologically and physiologically—are incredible and ought to serve as a warning.

We're designed to think in terms of plausibility structures and moral imaginations. The plausibility structure at play in culture is now built on sexual individualism; and the moral imagination in play is one that looks to eroticism and novelty as the highest human experience that fulfills our moral horizons and offers the potential for satisfaction.

As the church looks to minister in a landscape that looks more and more like a relational battlefield with casualties all around, perhaps the time has come for us to view the Christian sexual ethic less in terms of consumption and frequency; and more in terms of a moral imagination organized around one principle: the glory of God. Sexual pleasure, yes—but also covenantal faithfulness, long-suffering devotion, perseverance, sacrifice, and permanence—these are lasting products of the Christian moral imagination when applied to marriage.

Please hear me; this is not about reinvigorating prudeness. It is not about denying the beauty of erotic experience that God gives to us. It is, rather, about locating, securing, and anchoring these goods and virtues within marriage itself—where God *designed* it to occur. Frequent one-night stands are not beautiful, which means neither are they true or good. It tells of women being reduced to sexual receptacles whose value is leveraged on their *appearance*, not their *being*. It shows their longing for something more, but it also reveals their settling with this paradigm.

What is this experience we're seeing happen? It's replacement theology. Fornication, cohabitation, divorce, adultery, and Tinder—like every other deviation from God's sexual road map—is a *replacement theology*. It replaces biblical sexuality with the sexual zeitgeist of contemporary American culture. It is impossible for there not to be a sexual ethic guided by our deepest convictions. It's a question of whose ethic; and the ethic of progressivism, liberalism, and sexual revolution (rooted in the rejection of godly limits) is failing people in their sin. Why? Because sin fails people. It leaves them hollow. The *Vanity Fair* article screams hollowness. It narrates the silent screams of a generation habituated on cheapened notions of sexuality, the body, and deep relationship.

The breakdown of a healthy marriage culture and the endless quest to experience the blessings of marriage outside marriage itself is a guaranteed way to produce refugees of the sexual revolution—those who are burned out by the bitter fruits that the sexual revolution promises. The church must stand in the ruins of the sexual revolution and fill in the gap with a better story. Christians, admittedly, have not always lived up to that story. But let us encourage one another in faithfulness, hope, and thankfulness for a Savior that fills us with the power of the Holy Spirit to live lives of purity and faithfulness.

It doesn't always look like it; but even when Christians fail to live up to their own teachings, the moral-ethical imagination of Christianity is superior. It will win. The story of the octogenarian married couple, who can no longer engage in erotic pleasure, but hold one another dear at night for the sake of their personhood and commitment—that is beautiful. But sadly, it will take the loss, despair, hurt, and ugliness of a culture to recover the beauty of the Christian sexual ethic.

Marriage doesn't have to be dilapidated. It doesn't have to resemble the cynicism of marriages we see on TV, marriages like *Everybody Loves Raymond* where a passive adult man-boy, Raymond, treats his marriage as an annoying problem to be solved, rather than a gift to be protected.

The Christian church must offer something better to the culture around us. The church must be the vanguard that shows that marriage is a glorious service unto God.

German martyr Dietrich Bonhoeffer, while in Tegel prison for participating in an attempt to assassinate Adolf Hitler, wrote a marriage sermon in honor of his niece Renate Schleicher and Bonhoeffer's dearest friend, Eberhard Bethge. Bonhoeffer himself was engaged to be married while he wrote this letter. In it, Bonhoeffer concentrates on marriage as a "holy ordinance," packed with limitless potential to glorify God and bless the world.

> Marriage is more than your love for each other. It
> has a higher dignity and power, for it is God's holy
> ordinance, through which He wills to perpetuate the
> human race till the end of time. In your love you
> see only your two selves in the world, but in mar-
> riage you are a link in the chain of the generations,
> which God causes to come and to pass away to His
> glory, and calls into His kingdom. In your love, you
> see only the heaven of your own happiness, but in

marriage you are placed at a post of responsibility towards the world and mankind. Your love is your own private possession, but marriage is more than something personal—it is a status, an office. Just as it is the crown, and not merely the will to rule, that makes the king, so it is marriage, and not merely your love for each other, that joins you together in the sight of God and man. As you first gave the ring to one another and have now received it a second time from the hand of the pastor, so love comes from you, but marriage from above, from God. As high as God is above man, so high are the sanctity, the rights, and the promise of marriage of love. It is not your love that sustains the marriage, but from now on, the marriage that sustains your love.[15]

Discussion Questions

1. How is marriage presented in today's culture and ma media? How does this differ from the Bible's teachin and what should we say to the personal, emotional, an sentimental notions about marriage glorified in cultur

2. What are some of the arguments, attitudes, and tren that have resulted in the redefinition of marriage? Wh cultural assumptions now exist that might explain wh

Americans prepare more for the wedding day than for lifelong marriage?

3. How do plausibility structures and moral imaginations work together to bring about a cultural belief? What is the current plausibility structure and moral imagination informing the culture's understanding of marriage? What would a distinctively Christian view look like?

4. What is the difference between a covenant and contract? How does the Bible and specifically Jesus' teaching on marriage inform our understanding of the marriage covenant?

5. How can the Christian church offer a better picture of marriage to the culture? How can it counteract the silent screams and heartache left in the wake of the sexual revolution and offer a beautiful Scripture-centered and God-exalting alternative?

ADDITIONAL READING

This Momentary Marriage by John Piper

The Meaning of Marriage by Tim Keller

Sacred Marriage by Gary Thomas

The Mingling of Souls by Matt and Lauren Chandler

Marriage: Sex in the Service of God by Christopher Ash

Marriage Is: How Marriage Transforms Society and Cultivates Human Flourishing by Andrew T. Walker and Eric Teetsel

ACKNOWLEDGMENTS

TO THE MANY HANDS INSIDE AND OUTSIDE THE ERLC, WE thank you for your help and assistance on this book. The ERLC team provided joyful encouragement in the planning and execution of this series, and without them, it would never have gotten off the ground. We want to also personally thank Phillip Bethancourt who was a major visionary behind this project. We'd also like to thank Jennifer Lyell and Devin Maddox at B&H, our publisher, for their work in guiding us through this process.

ABOUT THE ERLC

THE ERLC IS DEDICATED TO ENGAGING THE CULTURE WITH the gospel of Jesus Christ and speaking to issues in the public square for the protection of religious liberty and human flourishing. Our vision can be summed up in three words: kingdom, culture, and mission.

Since its inception, the ERLC has been defined around a holistic vision of the kingdom of God, leading the culture to change within the church itself and then as the church addresses the world. The ERLC has offices in Washington, DC, and Nashville, Tennessee.

ABOUT THE
CONTRIBUTORS

Denny Burk is a professor of Biblical Studies at Boyce College, the undergraduate school of The Southern Baptist Theological Seminary in Louisville, Kentucky. He also serves as an associate pastor at Kenwood Baptist Church, which is in Louisville as well. He is the author of *What Is the Meaning of Sex?* (Crossway, 2013) and *Transforming Homosexuality* (P&R, 2015). He is a contributor to *Women in the Church*, 3rd ed. (Crossway, 2016) and *Four Views on Hell*, 2nd ed. (Zondervan, 2016).

Dean Inserra is pastor of City Church in Tallahassee, Florida. He is married and has three children.

Mary A. Kassian is an award-winning author and a distinguished professor of Women's Studies at The Southern Baptist Theological Seminary. She has published several books and Bible studies, including *Girls Gone Wise* and the *True Woman 101/201* curriculum. You can read her blog at GirlsGoneWise.com.

Dr. Dennis Rainey is a committed follower of Jesus Christ, husband of Barbara since 1972, father of six and Papa to twenty-two grandchildren (who all live too far away in his opinion), and has served in ministry since 1970. He serves as president and CEO of FamilyLife (familylife.com).

Andrew T. Walker serves as director of Policy Studies at the Ethics and Religious Liberty Commission.

NOTES

1. R. K. Bower and G. L. Knapp, "Marriage; Marry" in G. W. Bromiley, ed., *The International Standard Bible Encyclopedia, Revised* (Grand Rapids, MI: Wm. B. Eerdmans, 1979–1988), 3:262.

2. For an extensive study of Genesis chapters 1 to 3, which explores the created differences between man and woman, I suggest you do the Bible study *Divine Design: An Eight-Week Study on Biblical Womanhood* by Mary Kassian and Nancy Leigh DeMoss. (The content of the study is valuable for men too, as it also explores the meaning of manhood.)

3. David Platt, *Counter Culture* (Carol Stream, IL: Tyndale House Publishers, 2015), 138.

4. Ibid., 139.

5. Andrew T. Walker and Eric Teetsel, *Marriage Is: How Marriage Transforms Society and Cultivates Human Flourishing* (Nashville, TN: B&H Publishing Group, 2015), 1.

6. Wendy Wang and Kim Parker, "Record Share of Americans Have Never Married," *Pew Research Center's Social & Demographic Trends Project*, http://www.pewsocialtrends.org/2014/09/24/record-share-of-americans -have-never-married.

7. "Millennials in Adulthood," March 7, 2014, *Pew Research Center's Social & Demographic Trends Project*, http:///www.pewsocialtrends .org/2014/03/07/millennials-in-adulthood.

8. Ibid.

9. Jonel Aleccia, "The New Normal: Cohabitation on the Rise, Study Finds," *NBC*, April 3, 2013, http://vitals.nbcnews.com

/_news/2013/04/04/17588704-the-new-normal-cohabitation-on-th
-rise-study-finds?lite.

10. Erin O'Neill, "Steve Sweeney Claims Two-Thirds of Marriag
End in Divorce," *Politifact*, February 12, 2012, http://www.politifa
.com/new-jersey/statements/2012/feb/20/stephen-sweeney/steve-sweene
-claims-more-two-thirds-marriages-end. See also Scott Stanley, "Wh
Is the Divorce Rate, Anyway?: Around 42 Percent, One Schol
Believes," January 22, 2015, http://family-studies.org/what-is-th
-divorce-rate-anyway-around-42-percent-one-scholar-believes.

11. *Throuple*, *Wedlease*, and *Monogamish* are words mentioned i
Ryan T. Anderson's "Redefine Marriage, Debase Language?" *Nation*
Review Online, accessed August 8, 2013, http://www.nationalreview.co
/article/355295/redefine-marriage-debase-language-ryan-t-anderson.

12. Natalie Matthews, "What Gwyneth Paltrow's 'Consciou
Uncoupling' Really Means," *CNN*, March 26, 2014, http://www.cn
.com/2014/03/26/living/gwyneth-paltrow-conscious-uncoupling-el
/index.html.

13. Nancy Jo Sales, "Tinder and the Dawn of the 'Datir
Apocalypse,'" *Vanity Fair*, September 2015, http://www.vanityfair.co
/culture/2015/08/tinder-hook-up-culture-end-of-dating.

14. See http://www.nytimes.com/2016/06/19/fashion/profession
-cuddling.html?_r=0.

15. Dietrich Bonhoeffer, *Letters and Papers from Prison* (New Yor
NY: Touchstone, 1997), 42–43.